Table of Contents

Syllabus iv

Unit 1 All About You and Me
Lesson 1 New friends 2
Lesson 2 Neighborhoods 4
Mini-review 6
Lesson 3 Talents.......................... 8
Lesson 4 Our pets 10
Get Connected 12
Review 14

Unit 2 Our Lives and Routines
Lesson 5 School days 16
Lesson 6 Free time 18
Mini-review 20
Lesson 7 People I admire 22
Lesson 8 The weekend 24
Get Connected 26
Review 28

Unit 3 Sports and Activities
Lesson 9 Sports fun 30
Lesson 10 Sports equipment 32
Mini-review 34
Lesson 11 Off to camp 36
Lesson 12 At camp....................... 38
Get Connected 40
Review 42

Unit 4 My Interests
Lesson 13 I like music................... 44
Lesson 14 Let's look online.............. 46
Mini-review 48
Lesson 15 Our interests 50
Lesson 16 In and out of school 52
Get Connected 54
Review 56

Unit 5 Favorite Activities
Lesson 17 In San Francisco 58
Lesson 18 At the park 60
Mini-review 62
Lesson 19 At the beach 64
Lesson 20 At the store 66
Get Connected 68
Review 70

Unit 6 Entertainment
Lesson 21 Where are you going? 72
Lesson 22 Birthday parties 74
Mini-review 76
Lesson 23 Let's see a movie.............. 78
Lesson 24 In line at the movies 80
Get Connected 82
Review 84

Unit 7 What We Eat
Lesson 25 I'm hungry!.................... 86
Lesson 26 Picnic plans 88
Mini-review 90
Lesson 27 A snack........................ 92
Lesson 28 On the menu 94
Get Connected 96
Review 98

Unit 8 The Natural World
Lesson 29 World weather................. 100
Lesson 30 Natural wonders.............. 102
Mini-review 104
Lesson 31 World of friends 106
Lesson 32 International Day 108
Get Connected 110
Review 112

Games 114

Get Connected Vocabulary Practice 122

Theme Projects 126

Word List................................ 134

Unit 1 — All About You and Me

Lesson	Function	Grammar	Vocabulary
Lesson 1 New friends	Asking about others	Negative statements / Questions with the verb *be*	Name, age, country of origin, likes
Lesson 2 Neighborhoods	Describing your neighborhood	There is / There are … Is there a / Are there any …?	Recreational, commercial, and public places
Lesson 3 Talents	Describing someone's talents	*be good at*	Talents
Lesson 4 Our pets	Talking about likes and dislikes	*like* + a lot / very much / a little / *don't like* + very much / at all	Animals and adjectives to describe them
Get Connected	Reading • Listening • Writing		
Theme Project	Make a poster about things you like and things you're good at.		

Unit 2 — Our Lives and Routines

Lesson	Function	Grammar	Vocabulary
Lesson 5 School days	Describing daily routines	Simple present statements with *I*	Daily routines
Lesson 6 Free time	Asking about free-time activities	*Do you* + (verb) …?	Free-time activities
Lesson 7 People I admire	Talking about people's lives	Simple present statements with *I / he / she*	Activities
Lesson 8 The weekend	Talking about weekend activities	*doesn't*	Weekend activities
Get Connected	Reading • Listening • Writing		
Theme Project	Make a booklet about teachers in your school.		

Unit 3 — Sports and Activities

Lesson	Function	Grammar	Vocabulary
Lesson 9 Sports fun	Asking what sports someone does	*Does he / she* …?	Sports verbs
Lesson 10 Sports equipment	Talking about sports equipment	*They* + verb: statements / *Do they* + verb: questions	Sports equipment
Lesson 11 Off to camp	Talking about rules	Imperatives	Camp supplies
Lesson 12 At camp	Talking about when activities happen	*What time / When* …?	Camp activities
Get Connected	Reading • Listening • Writing		
Theme Project	Make a sports card.		

Unit 4 — My Interests

Lesson	Function	Grammar	Vocabulary
Lesson 13 I like music.	Talking about music preferences	*her / him / it / them*	Types of music
Lesson 14 Let's look online.	Asking about prices	*How much is / are* …?	Items in a natural science catalog
Lesson 15 Our interests	Talking about free-time activities	*like / don't like* + *to* (verb)	Free-time activities and interests
Lesson 16 In and out of school	Talking about habits and routines	Adverbs of frequency	Habits and daily activities
Get Connected	Reading • Listening • Writing		
Theme Project	Make a booklet of advertisements.		

revised edition

Connect

**Jack C. Richards
Carlos Barbisan**
com Chuck Sandy

Combo 2
Student's book

CAMBRIDGE
UNIVERSITY PRESS

University Printing House, Cambridge CB2 8BS, United Kingdom

One Liberty Plaza, 20th Floor, New York, NY 10006, USA

477 Williamstown Road, Port Melbourne, VIC 3207, Australia

314-321, 3rd Floor, Plot 3, Splendor Forum, Jasola District Centre, New Delhi – 110025, India

103 Penang Road, #05-06/07, Visioncrest Commercial, Singapore 238467

Cambridge University Press is part of the University of Cambridge.

It furthers the University's mission by disseminating knowledge in the pursuit of education, learning and research at the highest international levels of excellence.

www.cambridge.org
Information on this title: www.cambridge.org/9781107540040

© Cambridge University Press 2015

This publication is in copyright. Subject to statutory exception and to the provisions of relevant collective licensing agreements, no reproduction of any part may take place without the written permission of Cambridge University Press.

First published 2004
Second edition 2009
Revised edition 2015

20 19 18 17 16 15 14 13 12 11 10

Printed in Brazil by Forma Certa Grafica Digital LTDA

A catalogue record for this publication is available from the British Library

ISBN 978-1-107-54004-0 Combo 2

Additional resources for this publication at www.cambridge.org.br/connectarcade

Cambridge University Press has no responsibility for the persistence or accuracy of URLs for external or third-party internet websites referred to in this publication, and does not guarantee that any content on such websites is, or will remain, accurate or appropriate. Information regarding prices, travel timetables, and other factual information given in this work is correct at the time of first printing but Cambridge University Press does not guarantee the accuracy of such information thereafter.

Unit 5 Favorite Activities	Lesson	Function	Grammar	Vocabulary
	Lesson 17 In San Francisco	Describing vacation activities	Present continuous: affirmative statements	Vacation activities
	Lesson 18 At the park	Describing how someone is not following rules	Present continuous: negative statements	Rules at a park
	Lesson 19 At the beach	Asking what someone is doing	Present continuous: Yes / No questions	Beach activities
	Lesson 20 At the store	Asking what someone is doing	Present continuous: What questions	Store items
	Get Connected	Reading • Listening • Writing		
	Theme Project	Make a city guide for tourists.		

Unit 6 Entertainment	Lesson	Function	Grammar	Vocabulary
	Lesson 21 Where are you going?	Asking where someone is going	Where + (be) . . . going?	Entertainment events and adjectives to describe them
	Lesson 22 Birthday parties	Talking about special events	Simple present vs. present continuous	Favorite birthday activities
	Lesson 23 Let's see a movie.	Talking about types of movies to see	want / don't want + to (verb)	Types of movies
	Lesson 24 In line at the movies	Asking what someone looks like	What questions about people	Adjectives to describe appearance
	Get Connected	Reading • Listening • Writing		
	Theme Project	Make a weekend activity poster.		

Unit 7 What We Eat	Lesson	Function	Grammar	Vocabulary
	Lesson 25 I'm hungry!	Talking about food	Countable and uncountable nouns	Food
	Lesson 26 Picnic plans	Asking about quantities	How much / How many . . . ?	Picnic foods and utensils
	Lesson 27 A snack	Planning menus	some / any	Condiments
	Lesson 28 On the menu	Ordering from a menu	would like	Menu items
	Get Connected	Reading • Listening • Writing		
	Theme Project	Make a group menu.		

Unit 8 The Natural World	Lesson	Function	Grammar	Vocabulary
	Lesson 29 World weather	Talking about the weather	What's the weather like?	Adjectives to describe the weather
	Lesson 30 Natural wonders	Talking about outdoor activities	can (for possibility)	Water and land forms
	Lesson 31 World of friends	Asking who does different activities	Who + (verb) . . . ?	Languages and countries
	Lesson 32 International Day	Asking about personal information	What + (noun) . . . ?	Numbers 101 +
	Get Connected	Reading • Listening • Writing		
	Theme Project	Make an informational poster about a country.		

Lesson 1

New friends

1. Vocabulary review

A Read about the new students at Kent International School. Then listen and practice.

New Students at Kent International School

I'm Zach. I'm from the U.S., and I'm 12. I like baseball and volleyball.

Hello. I'm from Puerto Rico. My name is Ana, and I'm 13. I like movies and concerts.

My name is Tommy. I'm from Australia. I like music and comic books. I'm 13.

Hi. I'm Kate. I'm 13. I'm from Canada. I like computers and math.

Hello there! My name is Claudia. I'm 13. I'm from Colombia. My favorite sports are Ping-Pong and tennis.

My name is Rafael. I'm from Brazil. I like soccer and video games. I'm 13.

B Complete the chart with information from Part A.

Name	Age	Place	Likes
1. Claudia	13	Colombia	Ping-Pong and tennis
2.		Brazil	
3.		the U.S.	
4.			computers and math
5.		Puerto Rico	
6.	13		

2. Language focus review

A Review the language in the chart.

Negative statements / Questions with the verb *be*		
She**'s not** my art teacher.	They**'re not** my classmates.	My name**'s not** Anita.
Who**'s** she? She**'s** my math teacher.	Who are they? They**'re** my friends.	What**'s** your name? My name**'s** Ana.
It**'s not** in July.	It**'s not** in Brazil.	I**'m not** from São Paulo.
When**'s** your birthday? It**'s** in November.	Where**'s** San Juan? It**'s** in Puerto Rico.	Where are you from? I**'m** from San Juan.
He**'s not** fourteen.	Is he nice? Yes, he **is**. No, he**'s not**.	Are you in her class? Yes, I **am**. No, I**'m not**.
How old is he? He**'s** thirteen.		

B Complete the conversation. Listen and check. Then practice.

Zach Hi. _What's_ (What's / Where's) your name?

Ana My name's Ana. _____ (I'm / He's) from San Juan.

Zach Hi, Ana. My name's Zach. So, _____ (who's / where's) San Juan? _____ (Is / Are) it in Brazil?

Ana No, _____ (it's / it's not). It's in Puerto Rico.

Zach Oh, right. How old _____ (is / are) you, Ana?

Ana I'm 13. My birthday is in May. _____ (Where's / When's) your birthday?

Zach It's in June. Hey, _____ (who's / what's) she?

Ana _____ (They're / She's) my math teacher, Mrs. Archer.

Zach _____ (Are / Is) you in Ms. Kelley's science class?

Ana No, _____ (she's not / I'm not). I'm in Mr. Perez's class.

Zach _____ (Is / Are) he nice?

Ana Yes, he is. Actually, _____ (I'm / he's) my father.

3. Speaking

Think of a country, a hobby, or a school subject. Give clues. Your classmates guess.

You It's a country. It's not the U.S.
Classmate 1 Is it Peru?
You No, it's not.
Classmate 2 Is it Canada?
You Yes, it is!

All About You and Me 3

Lesson 2: Neighborhoods

1. Language focus review

What are Carson's and Johnny's neighborhoods like? Look at the pictures, and complete the sentences. Then listen and check.

There is / There are . . .
There's a park. / There's no park.
There are basketball courts. / There are no basketball courts.

Is there a / Are there any . . . ?
Is there a mall?
 Yes, there is. / No, there isn't.
Are there any stores?
 Yes, there are. / No, there aren't.

Carson's neighborhood

Johnny's neighborhood

Carson's neighborhood
1. _There's a_ beautiful park.
2. _____ tennis courts.
3. _____ basketball courts.

Johnny's neighborhood
4. _____ gym.
5. _____ many stores.
6. _____ big mall.

4 Unit 1

2. Listening

What other places are in Johnny's neighborhood? Listen and check (✓) the correct places.

- ✓ music store
- ☐ video arcade
- ☐ park
- ☐ basketball court
- ☐ swimming pool
- ☐ library
- ☐ school
- ☐ bookstore

3. Speaking

A Complete survey questions 1–6 with *Is there a* or *Are there any*. Write questions 7 and 8 with your classmates.

B Complete the survey for yourself. Then ask a classmate the questions.

Neighborhood Survey	You		Your classmate	
	Yes	No	Yes	No
1. _Is there a_ school?	☐	☐	☐	☐
2. _____ movie theaters?	☐	☐	☐	☐
3. _____ swimming pool?	☐	☐	☐	☐
4. _____ mall?	☐	☐	☐	☐
5. _____ restaurants?	☐	☐	☐	☐
6. _____ library?	☐	☐	☐	☐
7. _____	☐	☐	☐	☐
8. _____	☐	☐	☐	☐

Is there a school in your neighborhood?

Yes, there is.

C Tell your classmates about your neighborhood. Use the words below or your own ideas.

There's a big music store in my neighborhood. There are . . .

Lessons 1 & 2 Mini-review

1. Language check

A Read Kate's and Rafael's bulletin boards. Then write questions and answers.

1. **Q:** Where's Kate from?
   A: She's from Canada.
2. **Q:** Is Rafael from Brazil?
   A: _____
3. **Q:** _____
   A: It's in Canada.
4. **Q:** How old is Kate?
   A: _____
5. **Q:** _____
   A: He's 13.
6. **Q:** Where's São Paulo?
   A: _____
7. **Q:** Is Kate from Canada?
   A: _____
8. **Q:** Are Rafael and Kate in the same French class?
   A: _____

B Now ask and answer questions about Kate and Rafael.

Is Kate 13?   Yes, she is.

6   Unit 1

C What's in the stores on Main Street? Complete the questions and answers with *there is, there isn't, there are, there aren't, are there*, or *is there*.

1. *Is there* a bookstore on Main Street?

   Yes, _there is_. Read More! is a bookstore.

2. _____ any comic books in the bookstore?

   No, _____. _____ no comic books at the bookstore.

3. _____ a bicycle at Town Sports?

   Yes, _____. _____ soccer balls at the store, too.

4. _____ a music store on Main Street?

   Yes, _____. Notes is next to the bookstore.

5. _____ any video games in the computer store?

   No, _____. But, look, _____ some new laptops.

2. Listening

Monica describes her new school. Listen and check (✓) Yes or No.

	Yes	No
1. Is there a big library?	✓	
2. Is there a swimming pool?		
3. Are there any basketball courts?		
4. Are there any tennis courts?		
5. Is there a music room?		

Time for a Game?
See page 114.

All About You and Me 7

Lesson 3: Talents

1. Vocabulary

What are these students' talents? Write the sentences below the correct people. Then listen and practice.

- ☐ She's artistic. ☐ She's friendly. ☐ He's musical.
- ☐ She's athletic. ☑ He's funny. ☐ He's smart.

1. He can tell jokes.

   He's funny.

2. She can make friends easily.

3. He can speak three languages.

4. She can play a lot of sports.

5. He can play a lot of instruments.

6. She can draw great pictures.

2. Listening

A What do you think these students can do? Listen and check (✓) the correct activities.

1. Silvio: ☐ He can play basketball.   ☐ He can play video games.
2. Beth: ☐ She can play the guitar. ☐ She can play volleyball.
3. Tony: ☐ He can speak a lot of languages. ☐ He can dance.
4. Lina: ☐ She can play soccer. ☐ She can draw.

B Look at your answers to Part A. Write the word that describes each student.

1. *athletic*   2. _____   3. _____   4. _____

3. Language focus

A Who's good at soccer? Listen and practice.

Kate Hey, Claudia! You're good at soccer! You're really athletic!
Claudia Thanks.
Kate Who's that?
Claudia That's Zach.
Kate He's pretty good at soccer.
Claudia Yeah.
Kate Oh, no! Who's that?
Claudia Uh, that's Tommy. He's not good at soccer.
Kate No. But he can play a lot of instruments. He's very musical.

be good at

You're **good at** soccer.
He's **pretty good at** soccer.
Tommy's **not good at** soccer.

👍👍 good at
👍 pretty good at
👎 not good at

Tommy's = Tommy is

B What are you good at? Write sentences. Use the words below or your own ideas.

Subjects: English   history   math   science   art

Sports: volleyball   soccer   tennis   basketball

(good at) *I'm good at English.*

1. (good at) _____
2. (pretty good at) _____
3. (not good at) _____

C What are different students in your class good at? Tell your classmates.

> Heather's good at volleyball.

4. Pronunciation   Stress

Listen. Notice the stress in the sentences. Then listen again and practice.

I'm **good** at drawing. I'm **artistic**.	I'm **not** good at drawing. I'm **not** artistic.
I'm **good** at sports. I'm **athletic**.	I'm **not** good at sports. I'm **not** athletic.
He's **good** at the guitar. He's **musical**.	He's **not** good at the guitar. He's **not** musical.

All About You and Me

Lesson 4: Our pets

1. Vocabulary

 A Students describe their pets at the school pet show. Match the students to the correct texts. Then listen and practice.

☐ Binky and Cleo are boring. They're my brother's rabbits.

☐ Daisy is my cat. She's my favorite pet. She's really cute.

☐ Max is my dog. He's very active. I love dogs.

☐ Hans and Terry are my two spiders. They're very interesting.

1 Polly is my parrot. She can speak English. She's messy.

☐ I like my snake. His name is Ollie. He's not dangerous.

B Which pets in Part A do you think are great? Which pets are not so great? Complete the chart. Then tell your classmates.

Great	Why	Not so great	Why
dogs	cute		

> Dogs are great pets. They're cute.

> Snakes are not so great. They're boring.

2. Language focus

A Dora shows Ned the animals at the pet show. Listen and practice.

Dora Hey, Ned. Look at the cute cat. I like cats a lot.
Ned You do? I don't like cats very much. They're boring.
Dora But you like dogs, right?
Ned Yeah, they're really friendly.
Dora Well, I like dogs a little.
Ned Wow! Look at that snake over there.
Dora Ugh! I don't like snakes at all. They're dangerous.

> **like + a lot / very much / a little**
> **don't like + very much / at all**
>
> I **like** cats **a lot**.
> I **like** rabbits **very much**.
> I **like** dogs **a little**.
> I **don't like** spiders **very much**.
> I **don't like** snakes **at all**.

B Complete these sentences with the correct words. Then listen and check.

1. Rabbits are boring. I don't like rabbits ___at all___ (a little / at all).
2. Parrots are OK. I like parrots _____ (at all / a little).
3. Cats aren't very nice. I don't like cats _____ (a little / very much).
4. Dogs are cute. I like dogs _____ (a lot / at all).
5. Snakes are very bad pets. I don't like snakes _____ (a little / at all).
6. Spiders are interesting. I like spiders _____ (at all / very much).

3. Speaking

Learn what animals four of your classmates like and don't like.

You I like dogs a lot. How about you?
Classmate 1 I don't like dogs at all. I like cats very much.
Classmate 2 Well, I don't like cats at all. I like snakes a lot.
Classmate 3 Really? I don't like snakes at all. I like spiders a little.
Classmate 4 Hmm. I don't like . . .

All About You and Me

UNIT 1 Get Connected

Read

A Read the article quickly. Check (✓) the statements that are true.

☐ 1. The Web_Rats is a band from Brazil.
☐ 2. Jessica doesn't like the Web_Rats singers.
☐ 3. All members of Web_Rats write songs.

Web_Rats

Hi, I'm Jessica and this is my Web_Rats fan Web site. Web_Rats is a cool **boy band**. They're not famous, but I like their music a lot. They're not only a band, they're also friends. They all live in the same **apartment building** in Seattle, United States.

There are four boys in the band: William, Jasper, Hugh, and Brian. William is the oldest in the band. He's 24. Jasper and Hugh are 22. Brian, the youngest, is 21.

William is the **lead singer**, but all four boys write songs. Their most popular song on the Web – "Beautiful" – is about a **special** girl. Their other songs are about **typical** teenage things like friends.

All the boys are good at acting, too. All their **music videos** on the Web tell funny stories. The band has only a few hundred fans, but they're amazing. I love to watch them on the Internet!

More Vocabulary Practice? See page 122.

B T.14 Read the article slowly. Check your answers in Part A.

C Answer the questions.

1. What's the name of the band? *The name of the band is Web_Rats.*
2. Where are they from? _____
3. Are there five boys in the band? _____
4. Are the boys good at acting? _____
5. How old is Jasper? _____

That's not very important!

Listen

A 🎧 T.15 Alex and Anna talk about a band. Listen and answer the questions.

1. Is Anna on a science Web site? _No, she isn't._
2. Are the Plain White T's Anna's favorite band? _____
3. Are they from New York? _____
4. What's the lead singer's first name? _____
5. Are Alex and Anna classmates? _____

B What do you think? Write *I agree*, *I disagree*, or *I'm not sure*.

1. Fan Web sites are great. _____
2. The Plain White T's are a cool band. _____
3. Joss Stone is a great singer. _____
4. Music Web sites are interesting. _____
5. Homework is fun. _____

Your turn

Write

A Answer the questions about your favorite band.

1. What's the name of the band? _____
2. Where are they from? _____
3. Who are the members in the band? _____
4. How old are the band members? _____
5. What's your favorite song? _____

B Write an article for your fan Web site. Use the answers in Part A to help you.

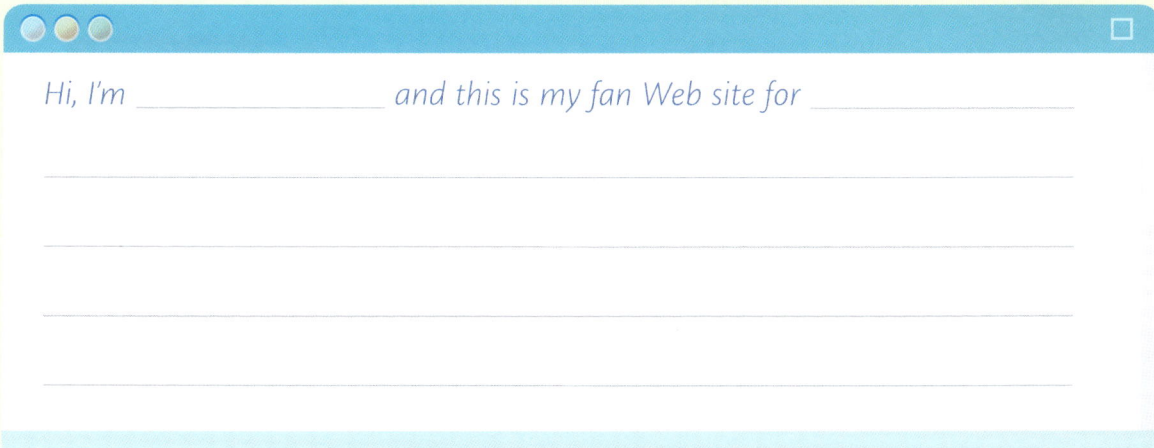

Hi, I'm _____ and this is my fan Web site for _____

UNIT 1 Review

Language chart review

The verb be			
Statements	**Wh- and How questions**	**Yes / No questions**	**Short answers**
I'm from Brazil. I'm not from Peru.	Where are you from?	Are you in my class?	Yes, I am. No, I'm not.
She's 12. She's not 13.	How old is she?	Is he from Australia?	Yes, he is. No, he's not.
We're at the mall. We're not at the park.	Where are you?	Are you brothers?	Yes, we are. No, we're not.
They're my friends. They're not my sisters.	Who are they?	Are they fun?	Yes, they are. No, they're not.

is not = isn't / 's not   are not = aren't / 're not

be good at
You're good at sports.   Jason's pretty good at music.   We're not good at science.
Jason's = Jason is

A Tom, Alex, and Eliza are in a new TV show. Complete the sentences.

Meet the kids from City Middle School

My _____name's_____ (name / name's) Tom Pond. _____ (I'm / He's) on a cool, new television show on Teen TV. The show is called *City Middle School*. My friends and I _____ (am / are) students at City Middle School. City Middle School _____ (is / are) in Lake City.

_____ (This is / These are) my friends. This is Alex. Alex is _____ (good is / good at) art. _____ (He's / She's) not good at math. _____ (They're / We're) in the same math class. Our teacher _____ (isn't / aren't) happy with Alex.

Say hello to Eliza. _____ (He's / She's) not from Lake City. _____ (She's / We're) Alex's cousin from Brazil. _____ (She / She's) pretty and very smart. Eliza's _____ (pretty good / is pretty) at sports, too.

14   Unit 1

B Write questions with the correct forms of *be*. Then look again at Part A, and answer the questions.

1. Tom's last name / Pond
   Q: Is Tom's last name Pond?   **A:** Yes, it is.
2. where / City Middle School
   Q: _____   **A:** _____
3. who / Alex and Eliza
   Q: _____   **A:** _____
4. Eliza / good at sports
   Q: _____   **A:** _____

Language chart review

There is / There are . . .	
There's a tennis court.	**There are** restaurants.
There's no basketball court.	**There are no** movie theaters.
Is there a mall?	**Are there any** music stores?
Yes, **there is.** / No, **there isn't.**	Yes, **there are.** / No, **there aren't.**

a lot / very much *a little / not at all*
I **like** science **a lot**.
I **like** geography **a little**.
I **don't like** math **very much**.
I **don't like** P.E. **at all**.

C Sam and Ann are at a pet store. Complete the conversation with *are, is, there's,* and *they're.*

Sam There ___are___ a lot of animals here!
Ann I know. _____ there a parrot?
Sam Yes, there _____ . Look!
Ann Oh, it's beautiful! And _____ a very cute cat.
Sam Cats aren't friendly.
Ann Oh, cats aren't bad. Look! _____ a black spider.
Sam Ugh! I don't like spiders at all. _____ there any dogs?
Ann Yes, there _____ . _____ in front of you.

D What do you think Sam and Ann say? Look again at Part C. Then write sentences with *like* or *don't like.*

1. (parrots / a lot)   **Ann** I like parrots a lot.
2. (cats / a little)   **Ann** _____
3. (cats / at all)   **Sam** _____
4. (dogs / a lot)   **Sam** _____

Time for the Theme Project?
See page 126.

All About You and Me

Lesson 5: School days

1. Vocabulary

A Read about Marcia's day. Then listen and practice.

Every day, I **get up** at 6:00 in the morning.

I **eat breakfast** at home.

Then I **go to school** with my brother.

I **eat lunch** with my friends in the cafeteria.

At 4:00, I **go home**.

Then I **do my homework**.

At 7:30, I **eat dinner** with my family.

Then I **watch TV**.

I **go to bed** at 10:00.

B Imagine you are Marcia. Complete her sentences with the correct words from Part A.

1. I _get up_ at 6:00 a.m.
2. I _____ at 8:00 p.m.
3. I _____ at 6:35 a.m.
4. I _____ at 4:30 p.m.
5. I _____ at 12:30 p.m.
6. I _____ at 10:00 p.m.
7. I _____ at 4:00 p.m.
8. I _____ at 7:30 p.m.

2. Language focus

 A How are Roberto's and Cindy's days different from Marcia's? Listen and practice.

Simple present statements with *I*
I go home after my guitar lesson.
I don't go home after school.
don't = do not

I don't go home after school.
I go home after my guitar lesson.
I don't watch TV after dinner.
I do my homework.

Roberto – Brazil

I don't go to school with my brother.
I go to school with my friends.
I don't eat dinner at 7:30.
I eat dinner at 6:00.

Cindy – Australia

B How about you? Is your day like Marcia's day? Write sentences.

(get up at 6:00) *I get up at 6:00, too.*   OR *I don't get up at 6:00. I get up at 7:00.*

1. (eat lunch with my friends) _____
2. (eat in the cafeteria) _____
3. (go home at 4:00) _____
4. (go to bed at 10:00) _____

C Now tell your classmates how your day is different from Marcia's day.

> I don't get up at 6:00. I get up at 7:00.

3. Listening

 Claudia talks about her day. What does she say? Listen and check (✓) the correct information.

1. I get up at   ✓ 7:00 a.m.   ☐ 8:00 a.m.
2. I go to school at   ☐ 8:30 a.m.   ☐ 9:00 a.m.
3. I eat lunch at   ☐ school.   ☐ home.
4. I go home at   ☐ 2:30.   ☐ 3:45.
5. I watch TV with   ☐ my brother.   ☐ my sister.

Our Lives and Routines 17

Lesson 6: Free time

1. Vocabulary

A Who does these free-time activities? Write **K** (Kate), **R** (Rafael), or **A** (Ana). Then listen and practice.

I collect stamps. _R_	I listen to music. ___	I take dance lessons. ___
I hang out at the mall. ___	I play video games. ___	I use the Internet. ___
I in-line skate. ___	I talk on the phone. ___	I watch videos and DVDs. ___

Kate

Rafael

Ana

B What do you do in your free time? Write two things you do and two things you don't do.

Things I do	Things I don't do
I . . .	I don't . . .

2. Language focus

Kate and Rafael take a survey. Complete the conversation. Listen and check. Then practice.

Kate Oh, look! A survey!
Rafael Cool. Let's take it.
Kate Um, do you collect trading cards?
Rafael Yes, I do.
Kate OK . . . Do you take piano lessons?
Rafael No, I don't.
Kate _Do_ you _use_ the Internet?
Rafael Yes, _____ .
Kate _____ you _____ TV?
Rafael No, _____ . But I watch videos.
Kate _____ you _____ to music?
Rafael _____ , I do. My favorite singer is Jennifer Lopez.
Kate _____ you _____ video games?
Rafael _____ , _____ . I play video games every weekend.

> **Do you + (verb) . . . ?**
> **Do you collect** trading cards?
> Yes, I do.
> No, I don't.

3. Speaking

A Read the survey. Write questions 8 and 9 with your classmates.

B Complete the survey for yourself. Then ask a classmate the questions.

What do you do in your free time?	You		Your classmate	
	Yes	No	Yes	No
1. Do you use the Internet?	☐	☐	☐	☐
2. Do you collect stamps?	☐	☐	☐	☐
3. Do you listen to music?	☐	☐	☐	☐
4. Do you play video games?	☐	☐	☐	☐
5. Do you talk on the phone?	☐	☐	☐	☐
6. Do you hang out at the mall?	☐	☐	☐	☐
7. Do you collect trading cards?	☐	☐	☐	☐
8. _____	☐	☐	☐	☐
9. _____	☐	☐	☐	☐

Do you use the Internet?   No, I don't.

Our Lives and Routines

Lessons 5 & 6 Mini-review

1. Language check

A Ricky writes about his day. What does he say? Write sentences.

6:30 a.m.
I get up at 6:30 a.m.

7:00 a.m.

8:30 a.m.

12:00 p.m.

3:00 p.m.

5:30 p.m.

7:00 p.m.

9:00 p.m.

10:00 p.m.

B You are going to interview Ricky. Look at Part A, and write four questions you can ask. Then act out the interview with a classmate.

1.
2.
3.
4.

You Do you get up at 6:30 a.m.?
Classmate Yes, I do.
You Do you play basketball at 7:00 p.m.?
Classmate No, I don't. I play basketball at 3:00 p.m.

20 Unit 2

C Circle the correct words to complete the conversation.

Carlos Hi, I'm Carlos.
Sally Hi, Carlos. My name's Sally.
Carlos Can I ask you questions for a survey?
Sally Uh, yeah.
Carlos (Are / Do) you in the 8th grade?
Sally Yes, I (am / do).
Carlos (Are / Do) you collect things?
Sally Yes, I (do / am). I collect stamps.
Carlos (Are / Do) you play video games after school?
Sally No, (I'm not / I don't). I listen to music.
Carlos Oh, who's your favorite singer?
Sally Well, I like Kylie Minogue, but (I'm not / I don't) like Justin Timberlake.

2. Listening

Sylvia, Kenji, Adam, and Cindy talk about their free time. Listen and check (✓) Yes or No.

T.21

1.	Sylvia	
	Yes	No
Read comic books	✓	☐
In-line skate	☐	☐
Hang out at the mall	☐	☐
Take dance lessons	☐	☐

2.	Kenji	
	Yes	No
Play video games	☐	☐
Collect stamps	☐	☐
Collect trading cards	☐	☐
Talk on the phone	☐	☐

3.	Adam	
	Yes	No
Take piano lessons	☐	☐
Play soccer	☐	☐
Hang out at the mall	☐	☐
Read books	☐	☐

4.	Cindy	
	Yes	No
Use the Internet	☐	☐
Watch DVDs	☐	☐
Play tennis	☐	☐
Talk on the phone	☐	☐

Time for a Game?
See page 115.

Lesson 7: People I admire

1. Vocabulary

Tommy admires his brother, Jordan. What does Jordan say about his life? Match the photos to the correct sentences. Then listen and practice.

- [ ] I go to concerts every Saturday.
- [ ] I have a piano, a bass, and an electric keyboard.
- [1] I live in an apartment.
- [ ] I play in a jazz band.
- [ ] I practice the piano every day.
- [ ] I work at Bradley Music School. I teach music to high school students.

2. Language focus

A Read what Tommy says. Study the language chart. Then listen and practice.

My brother, Jordan, is great. He works at Bradley Music School. He teaches the piano to students from all over the world. Jordan has a piano in his apartment, and he practices every day. At night, he plays in jazz clubs. He really loves music!

Simple present statements with *I / he / she*					Exception:
With *he* and *she*, add -s or -es to most verbs.					
I live	I work	I teach	I do	I go	I have
he lives	he works	he teaches	he does	he goes	he has
she lives	she works	she teaches	she does	she goes	she has

B Tommy also admires Esteban Cortazar. Complete Tommy's text with the correct forms of the verbs. Then listen and check.

I admire Esteban Cortazar. He's from Colombia, but he _____ (live) in Miami. Esteban is a fashion designer. He's talented, and he _____ (work) hard. He _____ (make) clothes for department stores. He _____ (go) to fashion shows, and he sees his own clothing!

3. Listening

Caroline Zhang is a famous skating star. Are these sentences true or false about her? Listen and write *T* (true) or *F* (false).

1. Caroline Zhang is American. __T__
2. She has a sister. _____
3. She lives with her family in New York. _____
4. She practices four days a week. _____
5. She plays the piano and the violin. _____
6. Her favorite singer is Jennifer Lopez. _____

4. Pronunciation -s endings

A Listen. Notice the *-s* endings. Then listen again and practice.

s = /s/	s = /z/	s = /ɪz/
takes	plays	practices
collects	goes	guesses

B Listen. Write these verbs in the correct columns: *lives*, *works*, *teaches*, *eats*, *watches*, and *has*.

s = /s/	s = /z/	s = /ɪz/

Our Lives and Routines

Lesson 8: The weekend

1. Vocabulary

A What do you do on the weekend? Check (✓) the correct boxes. Then listen and practice.

1. ☐ I **sleep late**.
   ☐ I don't sleep late.

2. ☐ I **eat out** with my family.
   ☐ I don't eat out with my family.

3. ☐ I **stay up late**.
   ☐ I don't stay up late.

4. ☐ I **go out** on Friday night.
   ☐ I don't go out on Friday night.

5. ☐ I **go to the movies**.
   ☐ I don't go to the movies.

6. ☐ I **stay home** on Sunday.
   ☐ I don't stay home on Sunday.

B Tell your classmates about your weekend. Use sentences from Part A.

> I sleep late. I eat out with my family. I don't . . .

2. Language focus

A Ana and her sister, Clara, do different things on the weekend. Listen and practice.

My sister and I are very different. On the weekend, I go out with my friends. I go to the movies, or I go to a concert. Clara doesn't go out at all. She stays home and watches videos. On Sunday, I don't sleep late. I get up at 7:30 a.m. Clara sleeps late. She gets up at 10:30 a.m.

doesn't
She doesn't go out on Friday night. **Clara doesn't go out** at all.
doesn't = does not

B Rafael and his brother, Luis, are different, too. Look at the photos. Are these sentences true or false? Write *T* (true) or *F* (false).

1. Luis goes out with his parents. __F__
2. Luis goes to concerts. _____
3. Rafael stays home. _____
4. Rafael goes to bed early. _____
5. Rafael watches videos in the living room. _____
6. Luis likes popcorn. _____

11:30 p.m.

Rafael

Luis

C Correct the false sentences in Part B. Then listen and check.

T.30

1. _Luis doesn't go out with his parents._
   He goes out with his friends.
2. _____
3. _____
4. _____

3. Speaking

A Read the survey. Write questions 7 and 8 with your classmates.

B Ask a classmate the questions.

What do you do on the weekend?	Your classmate	
	Yes	No
1. Do you sleep late?	☐	☐
2. Do you stay home?	☐	☐
3. Do you go to the movies?	☐	☐
4. Do you do your homework?	☐	☐
5. Do you go out with friends?	☐	☐
6. Do you play video games?	☐	☐
7. _____	☐	☐
8. _____	☐	☐

C Tell the class about your classmate's weekend activities.

> Carla eats out. She doesn't sleep late. She . . .

Our Lives and Routines

UNIT 2 Get Connected

Read

A Read the article quickly. Check (✓) the words you find.

☐ appears ☐ eats ☐ gives ☐ has ☐ helps ☐ lives ☐ lunch ☐ makes ☐ says

Quizlet

Do you have quizzes in school? Are they fun? If not, **check out** the quizzes on *Quizlet* – a cool Web site with lots of quizzes. *Quizlet* makes learning vocabulary words fun and exciting. And it's free!

The quizzes on *Quizlet* help students **review** languages (like English, Japanese, Spanish, and Korean) and school subjects (like history, geography, biology, and math). The quizzes are like games, so they're fun to do. Many students use *Quizlet* – over 30 million users per month on their Web site and apps.

Andrew Sutherland is the **creator** of *Quizlet*. *Quizlet* is very popular in schools around the world and it is also a very successful **company**. Andrew has a team that helps him with important things, like **marketing** and computer **software** questions about *Quizlet*. Andrew is really **smart** – he gives **interviews** and appears on many Web sites. He says that his passion is education.

More Vocabulary Practice? See page 122.

B 🎧 T.31 Read the article slowly. Check your answers in Part A.

C Are these statements true or false? Write *True* or *False*. Then correct the false statements.

1. *Quizlet* makes learning fun and exciting. *True.*
2. The quizzes on *Quizlet* are for languages only. _____
3. Few students use *Quizlet*. _____
4. *Quizlet* is a successful company, too. _____
5. Andrew has only one person that helps him. _____

We can study together.

A 🎧 T.32 Julia and Ben talk about their schedules. Listen and check (✓) the correct words.

1. Ben has a lot of	☐ homework.	✓ quizzes.
2. Ben doesn't have	☐ a Spanish	☐ an English quiz on Wednesday.
3. On Monday Julia has	☐ dance class.	☐ soccer practice.
4. On Tuesday Julia doesn't have any	☐ homework.	☐ extra classes.
5. Julia doesn't like	☐ math.	☐ English.

B What do you think? Write *I agree, I disagree,* or *I'm not sure.*

1. Quizzes are fun. _____
2. It's good to use computers in class. _____
3. It's good to study with classmates. _____
4. Math is important. _____

Your turn

A Think of a person who does interesting things. Use the words in the box or your own ideas to complete the web about one person.

collect eat go hang out have play read take use watch work write

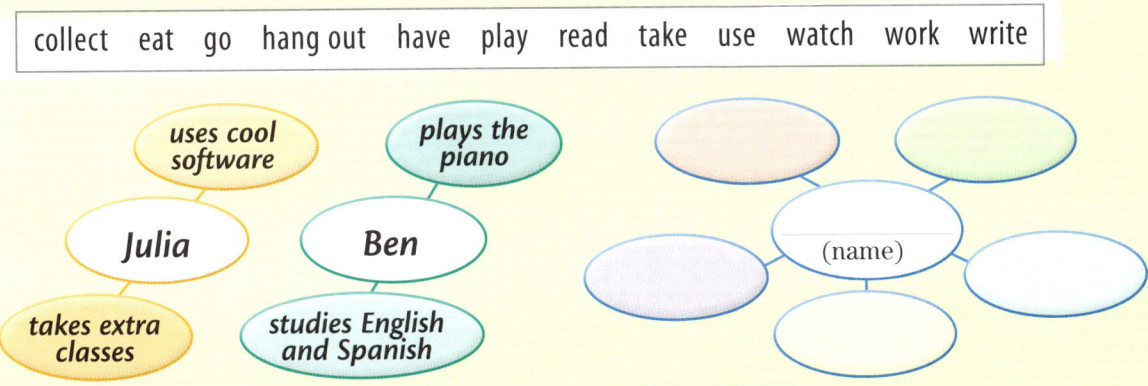

B Write a paragraph about an interesting person. Use your ideas in Part A to help you.

_____ *does a lot of interesting things. He* _____

UNIT 2 Review

Language chart review

Simple present		
Statements: *I / He / She*	**Yes / No questions:** *Do you . . . ?*	**Short answers**
I take piano lessons. **I don't take** violin lessons. **He lives** in an apartment. **He doesn't live** in a house. **She gets up** late. **She doesn't get up** early.	**Do you take** piano lessons?	Yes, I do. No, I don't.

doesn't = does not

A Carly writes a fan letter to a Brazilian musician. Complete Carly's letter and the reply. Use the verbs in the box.

do	don't live	have	live
doesn't have	has	listens to	play

Dear Jorge,

How are you? This letter is from my grandfather and me. I _have_ all your CDs. My grandfather _doesn't have_ your CDs, but he _____ all of your father's music. Your father, João Barbosa, is his favorite musician. He _____ his music every day. Can you please answer some questions?

_____ you _____ in São Paulo? _____ you _____ any brothers and sisters? _____ you _____ another instrument?

You're the best!

Best regards,

Carly

Dear Carly,

Hi! Here is a picture of my dad and me playing.

No, I _____ in São Paulo.
I _____ in Rio de Janeiro.
Yes, I _____ a big family.
I have two brothers and three sisters!

Yes, I _____ piano.

Thanks for your letter! And thanks to your grandfather, too!

Jorge

B Write *Do you* questions. Use Part A to help you. Then write short answers using your own information.

1. (live / Spain)
   Q: <u>Do you live in Spain?</u>   A: <u>Yes, I do.</u>   OR <u>No, I don't.</u>

2. (listen / CDs)
   Q: _____   A: _____

3. (have / brothers and sisters)
   Q: _____   A: _____

4. (sing / songs in English)
   Q: _____   A: _____

C Read about Antonio. Then correct the sentences.

I'm Antonio Burgos. I live in Buenos Aires, Argentina, with my parents and my little sister, Monica. I go to a small school in the city. My first language is Spanish, but I speak English, too. In my free time, I play video games and listen to music. I don't like rap music very much, but I love rock. On weekends, I hang out at the park with my friends, but I eat dinner with my family.

1. Antonio lives in the United States.
   <u>Antonio doesn't live in the United States. He lives in Argentina.</u>

2. He has a little brother.
   _____

3. He speaks French and Portuguese.
   _____

4. Antonio plays soccer and watches TV.
   _____

5. He likes rap music.
   _____

6. He hangs out at the mall on weekends.
   _____

Time for the Theme Project?
See page 127.

Lesson 9 — Sports fun

1. Vocabulary

A Who does these sports, Claudia or Zach? Listen and write **C** (Claudia) or **Z** (Zach).
T.33

I surf. _____

I do karate. __C__

I skateboard. _____

I go biking. _____

I water-ski. _____

I play baseball. _____

I swim. _____

I ski. _____

B Listen and practice.
T.34

C What sports do you do? What sports don't you do? Write sentences.

Sports I do	Sports I don't do
I skateboard.	I don't ski.

2. Language focus

Does he / she . . . ?
Does he do karate?
Yes, he does.
No, he doesn't.

A Claudia and Zach talk about a new student. Listen and practice.

Claudia Hey, that guy's new. Who is he?
Zach That's Chris.
Claudia Does he like sports?
Zach Well, . . .
Claudia Does he do karate?
Zach No, he doesn't.
Claudia Does he play baseball?
Zach No, he doesn't.
Claudia Does he surf?
Zach Uh . . . yes, he does. He surfs the Internet!

B Chris and Zach talk about Claudia. Complete the conversation. Listen and check. Then practice.

Chris Wow! Your friend Claudia is good at basketball.
Does she play other sports?
Zach _____, she does. She's very athletic.
Chris _____ she play soccer?
Zach Yes, she _____ . She likes it very much.
Chris _____ she have a gym partner?
Zach No, she _____ .
Chris Hey, maybe she can be my partner!
She can help me!

3. Pronunciation Intonation

Listen. Notice the rising intonation in *Yes / No* questions. Then listen again and practice.

Does he swim?   Does he surf?   Does she do karate?   Does she play soccer?

4. Speaking

Think of a sports star. Give clues. Your classmates guess. Use the correct intonation.

Classmate 1 Does he ski? **You** No, he doesn't.
Classmate 2 Does he skateboard? **You** Yes, he does.
Classmate 3 Is he American? **You** Yes, he is.
Classmate 4 Is he Ryan Scheckler? **You** Yes, he is!

Sports and Activities

Lesson 10: Sports equipment

1. Vocabulary

 A Where does Claudia wear this sports equipment? Write the correct word next to each body part. Then listen and practice.

1. head _helmet_
2. eye(s) _____
3. hand(s) _____
4. knee(s) _____
5. foot / feet _____

☐ glove(s)
☐ goggles
☐ ski boot(s)
☐ knee pad(s)
☑ helmet

B What sports equipment do these athletes wear? Make guesses and complete the chart.

A skateboarder	A skier	A cyclist
helmet		

32 Unit 3

2. Language focus

A Claudia's little brother, Oscar, helps get the sports equipment. Listen and practice.

Claudia Oscar, can you help me, please? I need the sports equipment for the swim team.
Oscar Sure! Here is the helmet . . .
Claudia Huh? Swimmers don't wear helmets.
Oscar Um, do they wear gloves?
Claudia No, they don't. They wear goggles.
Oscar Oh! Um, do swimmers wear knee pads?
Claudia No, they don't. They don't wear knee pads!
Oscar Sorry. I don't know a lot about sports.
Claudia No kidding!

They + (verb): statements

They wear goggles.
They don't wear helmets.

Do they + (verb): questions

Do they wear gloves?
  Yes, they do.
  No, they don't.

B How much do you know about sports? Answer the questions. Listen and check. Then practice.

1. **Q:** Do skiers wear sneakers?
   A: *No, they don't. They wear ski boots.*

2. **Q:** Do soccer players have uniforms?
   A: _____

3. **Q:** Do baseball players play on a court?
   A: _____

4. **Q:** Do cyclists wear hats?
   A: _____

5. **Q:** Do skateboarders use knee pads?
   A: _____

6. **Q:** Do basketball players play on a field?
   A: _____

3. Listening

Claudia plays a game with Oscar. What athletes do they talk about? Listen and number the pictures.

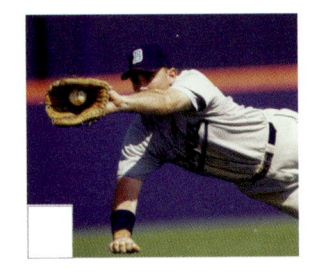

Sports and Activities

Lessons 9 & 10 — Mini-review

1. Language check

A Look at the pictures. Write sentences with *wear* or *don't wear*.

1. *They wear baseball gloves.* (glove)
   They don't wear boots. (boots)

2. _____ (knee pads)
   _____ (goggles)

3. _____ (hats)
   _____ (uniforms)

4. _____ (helmets)
   _____ (goggles)

B Complete the sentences with the words in the box.

☐ eyes ☐ feet ✓ hands ☐ head ☐ knees

1. Cyclists wear gloves on their _hands_ .
2. Swimmers wear goggles over their _____ .
3. Skateboarders wear pads on their _____ .
4. Skiers wear boots on their _____ .
5. You wear a helmet on your _____ .

Unit 3

C Complete the interview with Angela Moya, a champion skateboarder. Use *do*, *does*, *don't*, and *doesn't*.

Sports for Kids

Interviewer Hi, Angela. Nice to meet you.
Angela Hi!
Interviewer Angela, we know you love sports. Do your parents like sports, too?
Angela Yes, they ___do___ . My dad likes outdoor sports.
Interviewer _____ he go biking?
Angela Yes, he _____ . He goes biking every day, actually.
Interviewer And your mother? _____ she go biking, too?
Angela No, she _____ . She swims and water-skis.
Interviewer And your sisters? _____ they skateboard?
Angela No, they _____ . They like team sports, like soccer and basketball.
Interviewer What about you? _____ you play team sports?
Angela No, I _____ . I skateboard, of course. And I run every day, too.

Champion Skateboarder
Angela Moya, 13 – Denver, Colorado

2. Listening

A Listen to more of the interviewer's questions from Exercise 1C. Check (✓) the correct responses.

1. ☑ No, they don't. They don't like water sports.
   ☐ Yes, they do. They play every weekend.

2. ☐ Yes, I do. It's fun.
   ☐ Yes, they do. They love the mountains.

3. ☐ No, it isn't.
   ☐ Yes, she does. She's a great player.

4. ☐ Yes, she does. She's on the team.
   ☐ Yes, she does. She likes it very much.

5. ☐ Yes, we do. Every summer.
   ☐ No, he doesn't. He doesn't like the water.

B Now listen to the complete interview in Part A. Check your answers.

Time for a Game?
See page 116.

Sports and Activities

Lesson 11 — Off to camp

1. Vocabulary

A Megan packs to go to camp. Match the items in Megan's room to the correct items on the checklist. Then listen and practice.

Camp Coby Camper Checklist
Bring:
blanket ____
bug repellent __1__
flashlight ____
hiking boots ____
pillow ____
raincoat ____
sleeping bag ____
soap ____
sunscreen ____
towel ____

Remember:
No cell phones
No computers
No radios
No video games

B Complete the sentences with the words in Part A.

1. The _bug repellent_ is on the desk.
2. The _____ is under the desk.
3. The _____ is on the desk.
4. The _____ is on top of the blanket.
5. The _____ is next to the bed.
6. The _____ is on the bed.
7. The _____ is under the bed.
8. The _____ is under the chair.
9. The _____ is on the chair.
10. The _____ are next to the desk.

2. Language focus

A Megan's mother helps Megan pack for camp. Listen and practice.

Imperatives

Hurry up.
Don't stay up late.

Megan Let's go. Hurry up, Mom.
Mom Just a minute, Megan. Don't wear a dress. Wear something comfortable.
Megan But this *is* comfortable, Mom.
Mom Fine, Megan, but read the checklist again. It says "No computers." Leave your computer at home, please.
Megan But I use my computer at night, Mom.
Mom I know, but there are camp activities at night.
Megan Oh, good! I can stay up until midnight.
Mom No, Megan! It's camp. Don't stay up late.
Megan Mom, please stop. Camp is supposed to be fun!

B Look at the checklist in Exercise 1A. Can you guess the Camp Coby rules? Complete the rules. Then listen and check.

Camp Coby Rules

1. *Don't play* video games. (play / don't play)
2. _____ hiking boots. (wear / don't wear)
3. _____ to the radio. (listen / don't listen)
4. _____ cell phones. (bring / don't bring)
5. _____ computers. (use / don't use)
6. _____ a flashlight. (bring / don't bring)
7. _____ sunscreen. (use / don't use)

3. Speaking

Write four crazy rules for Camp Coby. Close your book and tell your rules to your classmates. Who has the craziest rules?

Get up at 11:00 every day.

Sports and Activities 37

Lesson 12 At camp

1. Vocabulary

A Look at the Camp Coby Web site. Match the photos to the correct activities. Then listen and practice.

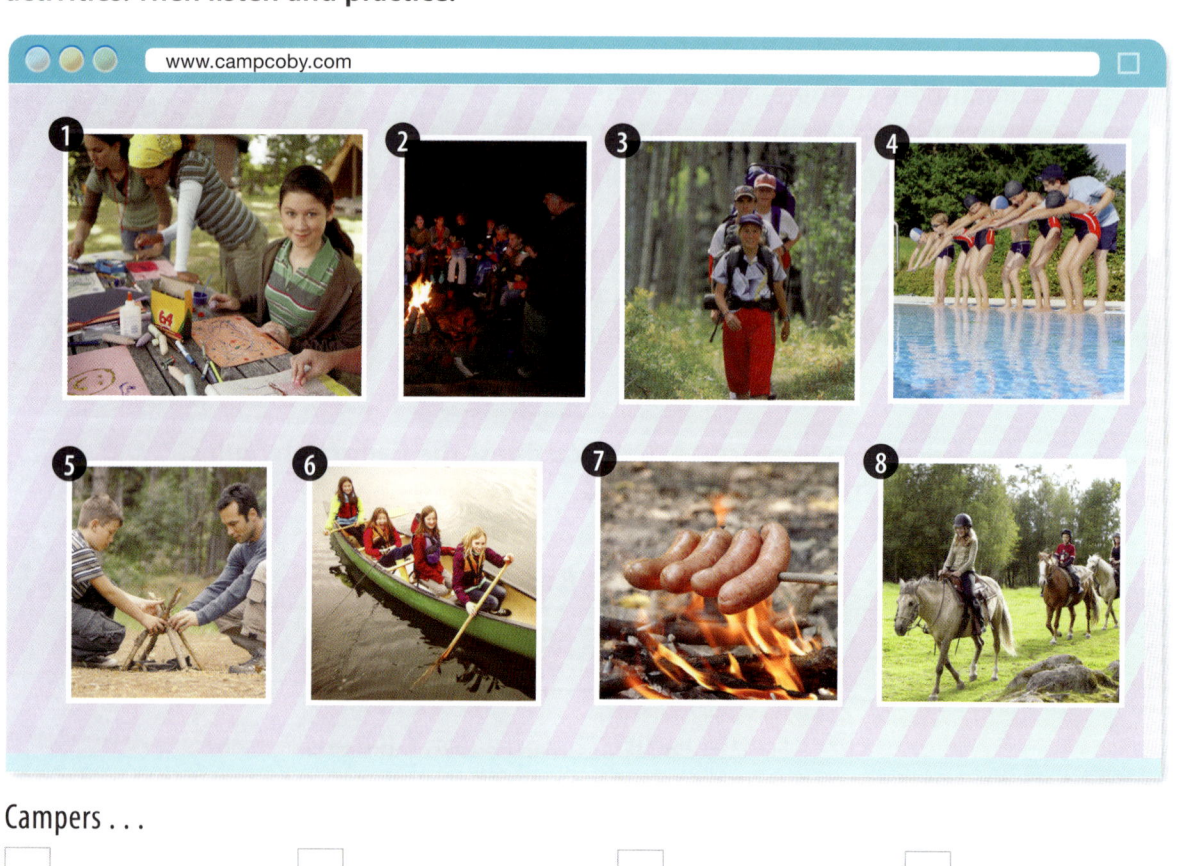

www.campcoby.com

Campers . . .

- [ ] cook hot dogs.
- [ ] go canoeing.
- [ ] go hiking.
- [ ] take swimming lessons.
- [1] do arts and crafts.
- [ ] go horseback riding.
- [ ] make a campfire.
- [ ] tell stories.

B What do campers do at Camp Coby? Listen and write an activity for each time.

Time	Activity
8:00 a.m.	*They go horseback riding.*
10:00 a.m.	
1:15 p.m.	
3:30 p.m.	
4:45 p.m.	
8:15 p.m.	
8:30 p.m.	
9:00 p.m.	

2. Language focus

A Megan's parents read her letter. Listen and practice.

Mom Wow! Megan is very busy at Camp Coby!
Dad Great! What time does she get up?
Mom She gets up at 6:30.
Dad Wow. Campers get up early. What do they do every day?
Mom Let's see. They do arts and crafts, they go canoeing, they go hiking . . .
Dad When do they go hiking?
Mom They go hiking in the afternoon.
Dad It sounds like fun! Can parents go to camp, too?

What time / When . . . ?

What time does Megan get up?
  She gets up **at 6:30**.
  At 6:30.
When do they go hiking?
  They go hiking **in the afternoon**.
  They go hiking **at 2:00**.
  At 2:00.

in the morning = about 5 a.m. to 12 p.m.
in the afternoon = about 12 p.m. to 6 p.m.
in the evening = about 6 p.m. to 10 p.m.
at night = about 10 p.m. to 5 a.m.

B Look at the schedule in Exercise 1B. Write questions about Megan. Use *When* or *What time*. Listen and check. Then practice.

1. **Q:** *When does Megan take swimming lessons?* OR
   What time does Megan take swimming lessons?
   A: She takes swimming lessons at 10:00.

2. **Q:** _____
   A: She goes canoeing in the afternoon.

3. **Q:** _____
   A: At 4:45.

4. **Q:** _____
   A: At 8:15.

5. **Q:** _____
   A: She tells stories in the evening.

3. Listening

Listen to the activities at another camp – Camp Oakley. When do campers do these activities? Check (✓) the correct times of the day.

	In the morning	In the afternoon	In the evening	At night
1. go hiking	✓	☐	☐	☐
2. go horseback riding	☐	☐	☐	☐
3. do arts and crafts	☐	☐	☐	☐
4. take swimming lessons	☐	☐	☐	☐
5. tell stories	☐	☐	☐	☐

Sports and Activities

UNIT 3 Get Connected

Read

A Read the article quickly. Check (✓) the main idea.

☐ 1. Missy Franklin is a famous world champion.

☐ 2. Missy Franklin doesn't have a big family.

☐ 3. Missy Franklin is a talented swimmer and a positive role model, too.

Missy Franklin

Meet the very talented Melissa Jeanette Franklin! Her nickname is Missy, and she is a tall and athletic **world champion** swimmer. She has four Olympic gold **medals** and six World Championship gold medals. Missy is from the United States, and she lives in Berkeley, California. Her parents are Canadian. Missy doesn't have any brothers or sisters. She's an **only child**.

Missy loves swimming, and she trains two hours a day. She is a hardworking athlete! She knows that being a champion takes constant practice. It means swimming every day! She is always in the water. Because of pool chlorine, she wears goggles to protect her eyes. But Missy doesn't only swim. She is a great person, too.

Missy likes to help people. She is involved in volunteer activities. She likes to be a positive **role model** for young athletes in all sports. Her **teammates** think she's awesome. They say that she always has a smile on her face. So, what do you think? Isn't she a cool person? Do you like to help people, too?

More Vocabulary Practice? See page 123.

B 🎧 T.52 Read the article slowly. Check your answer in Part A.

C Answer the questions.

1. Does Missy like swimming? _Yes, she does._
2. Does she have a sister? _____
3. Does she practice swimming every day? _____
4. Does she wear any special sports equipment? _____
5. Does she need to wear a helmet? _____

She's good at two different things.

Listen

A Sam and Amy talk about Serena Williams. Listen and answer the questions.

1. Does Serena have a sister? _Yes, she does._
2. Does Venus design clothes? _____
3. Does Serena have a company? _____
4. Does her company have offices in Paris? _____
5. Is Amy at Sam's house? _____

B What do you think? Answer the questions.

1. Do you think tennis matches on TV are interesting? _____
2. Do you think it's easy to be athletic? _____
3. Do you think fashion design is a cool subject? _____
4. Do you think it's important to be good at two things? _____

Your turn

Write

A Think about a person who is good at two things. Answer the questions.

1. What's his / her name? _____
2. Who is he / she? A friend? A family member? A classmate? A teacher?
   _____
3. What does he / she do? _____
4. What other special thing can he / she do? _____
5. What's he / she like? _____

B Write a paragraph about a person who's good at two things. Use the answers in Part A to help you.

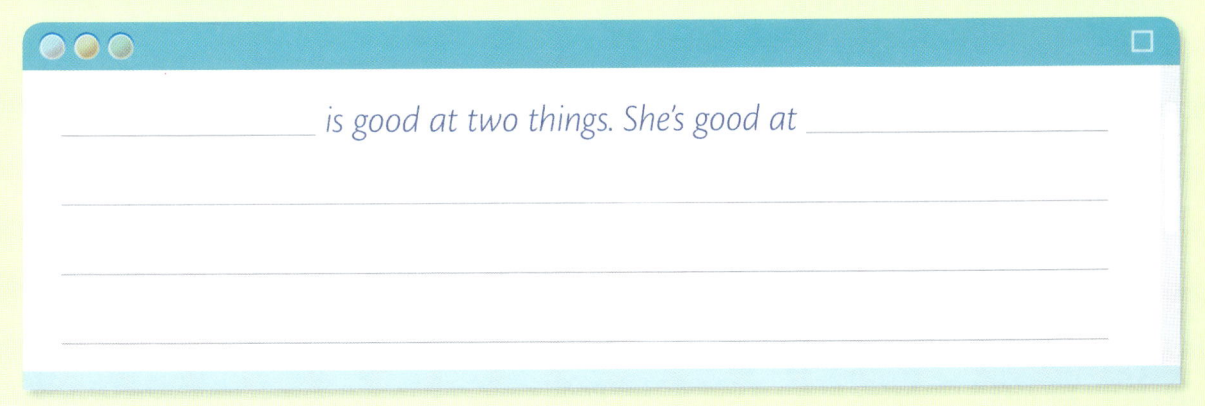

_____ is good at two things. She's good at _____

Sports and Activities

UNIT 3 Review

Language chart review

Simple present		
They + (verb): statements	*Yes* / *No* questions: he / she / they	Short answers
Skateboarders **wear** helmets. They **don't wear** goggles.	**Does** he **swim**?	Yes, he does. No, he doesn't.
	Does she **do** karate?	Yes, she does. No, she doesn't.
	Do they **like** sports?	Yes, they do. No, they don't.

A The basketball team at Ryder School is very unusual. Look at the picture. Write *Do* or *Does* questions about the team. Use the correct forms of the verbs. Then answer the questions.

1. the players / play in the gym
   Q: <u>Do the players play in the gym?</u>   **A:** <u>No, they don't. They play in the cafeteria.</u>

2. the players / wear sneakers
   Q: _____   **A:** _____

3. the coach / wear goggles
   Q: _____   **A:** _____

4. player 2 / have a basketball
   Q: _____   **A:** _____

5. players 4 and 5 / listen to music
   Q: _____   **A:** _____

42 Unit 3

Language chart review

Imperatives	What time . . . ?	When . . . ?
Read a book. **Don't play** video games.	**What time** does he go hiking? He goes hiking **at 5:00**. At 5:00.	**When** do they use their computers? They use their computers **at night**. They use their computers **at 7:30**. At 7:30.

B Write imperatives with the verb phrases in the box.

☐ go to bed early ☐ swim there ☑ talk on your cell phone ☐ use sunscreen

1. *Don't talk on your cell phone.*
2. _____
3. _____
4. _____

C Two swimming coaches are talking about their teams. Complete the conversation with the sentences in the box.

☐ a. What time do they eat breakfast?
☑ d. Does Maggie Ferre swim on your team?
☐ b. So, when do your swimmers practice?
☐ e. What about her brother, Joe? Does he swim, too?
☐ c. What time do they swim?

Coach Sala   *d*
Coach Hanes   Yes, she does.
Coach Sala   _____
Coach Hanes   No, he doesn't. He's on the baseball team.
Coach Sala   _____
Coach Hanes   They practice in the morning.
Coach Sala   _____
Coach Hanes   Very early. At 6:30.
Coach Sala   _____
Coach Hanes   After they practice. At 8:00.

Time for the Theme Project? See page 128.

Sports and Activities 43

Lesson 13: I like music.

1. Vocabulary

A Listen to these kinds of music and practice.

classical   country   hip-hop   jazz   pop   reggae   rock

B Work with your classmates. Look at the photos, and complete the labels with words from Part A. Then listen and practice.

Music Magazine
Top Musicians of the Year

Kanye West
Joshua Bell
Sean Paul
Pink

1. _hip-hop_ singer
2. _____ musician
3. _____ singer
4. _____ singer

Jon Bon Jovi
The Dixie Chicks
Wynton Marsalis

5. _____ singer
6. _____ group
7. _____ musician

C Learn what kinds of music four of your classmates like and don't like.

You Yumi, what's your favorite kind of music?
Classmate 1 My favorite kind of music is jazz.
You What's your favorite kind of music, Leah?
Classmate 2 My favorite kind of music is . . .

2. Language focus

A Daisy Fines of *Music Magazine* interviews Ana. Listen and practice.

> **Daisy** So, Ana, what's your favorite kind of music?
> **Ana** Well, I think country is cool. The Dixie Chicks are great. I really like them.
> **Daisy** I do, too! They're a *great* country group! How about other kinds of music? Do you like jazz?
> **Ana** No, I don't like it at all.
> **Daisy** Really? What about Wynton Marsalis? A lot of people like him.
> **Ana** Well, yeah, I guess he's OK. But I don't listen to much jazz. I like country, pop, and rock.
> **Daisy** Do you listen to Pink?
> **Ana** Yes! I love her! She's my favorite pop singer.

her / him / it / them
She's great. I like **her** a lot. He's my favorite. I like **him** a lot.
Hip-hop is cool. I like **it**. They're boring. I don't like **them** at all.

B What do other teens tell Daisy? Complete their sentences with *her*, *him*, *it*, or *them*. Then listen and check.

1. Pop music isn't interesting. I don't like ___it___ .
2. The Dixie Chicks are cool. I like _____ a lot.
3. Kanye West is my favorite hip-hop singer. I love _____ .
4. Classical music is boring. I don't like _____ at all.
5. Pink is an interesting singer. I like _____ .
6. Sean Paul is great. I love _____ .

3. Speaking

Complete questions 6, 7, and 8. Then ask a classmate the questions.

Do you like . . . ?	A lot	A little	Not at all
1. jazz	☐	☐	☐
2. country	☐	☐	☐
3. rock	☐	☐	☐
4. hip-hop	☐	☐	☐
5. reggae	☐	☐	☐
6. _____ (male singer)	☐	☐	☐
7. _____ (female singer)	☐	☐	☐
8. _____ (group)	☐	☐	☐

Peter, do you like jazz?

No, I don't like it at all.

Lesson 14: Let's look online.

1. Vocabulary

A Look at some items in the *Discover Your World* online catalog. Then listen and practice.

Discover Your World ONLINE STORE

1. star map — $17.50
2. telescope — $49.95
3. radio-controlled airplane — $96.99
4. travel vest — $52.06
5. nature puzzles — $9.89 each
6. adventure DVDs — $34.79 each
7. science kit — $60.00
8. wall calendars — $16.00 each

B Look at the items and prices in Part A. Then listen and practice.

C Practice saying the items and prices with a classmate.

- The travel vest.
  - It's fifty-two-oh-six. OR It's fifty-two dollars and six cents.

- The nature puzzles.
  - They're nine eighty-nine each. OR They're nine dollars and eighty-nine cents.

- The wall calendars.
  - They're sixteen dollars each.

2. Language focus

A Ben talks to Tina about things in the online catalog. Listen and practice.

> **How much is / are . . . ?**
> **How much is** it?
> It's **$96.99**.
> **How much are** the puzzles?
> They're **$9.89** each.

Ben Hey! This is a great Web site!
All these things are cool.
There's a great radio-controlled airplane.
Tina Really? Radio controlled? How much is it?
Ben It's $96.99.
Tina That's almost a hundred dollars!
Ben I know. I like these nature puzzles, too.
Tina How much are they?
Ben They're $9.89 each.
Tina Hmm. That's not very expensive.

B Complete the rest of the conversation. Listen and check. Then practice.

Ben Wow. I like this telescope.
Tina _How much is_ it?
Ben _____ $49.95. And there's an interesting star map, too. I can study the stars!
Tina _____ the star map?
Ben _____ $17.50. And these adventure DVDs are exciting.
Tina And _____ the adventure DVDs, Ben?
Ben Well, _____ $34.79 each.
Tina You like a lot of things, Ben. Too bad you don't have a lot of money!

3. Listening

Ben and Tina compare prices in their catalogs. Listen and write the prices in the chart.

	Watch	T-shirts	Camera	Hiking boots	Backpack
Ben's online catalog	$39.99				
Tina's catalog	$29.99				

My Interests

Lessons 13 & 14 Mini-review

1. Language check

A Bryan and Ashley shop for a birthday present for their friend, Matt. Complete the conversation with the correct words. Then practice.

Bryan It's Matt's birthday on Sunday. What can we get ___him___ (her / him)?
Ashley How about a CD? Does he like reggae?
Bryan No, he doesn't like _____ (it / them) at all.
Ashley Well, what about pop? Does he like pop?
Bryan Yes. Actually, he loves _____ (it / them). His favorite singer is Pink.
Ashley Really? I like _____ (him / her), too.
Bryan Oh, look. Here's a CD by the Dixie Chicks.
Ashley Does Matt like the Dixie Chicks?
Bryan Yes, he loves _____ (it / them).
Ashley Great. How much _____ (is / are) the CD?
Bryan _____ (It's / They're) $13.95.
Ashley OK. Let's buy _____ (it / them).

B Bryan asks Ashley about the prices of other things in the music store. Write their questions and answers.

- electric guitar $98.99
- DVDs $32.99
- T-shirt $8.99
- posters $10.99 each

1. **Bryan** _How much is the electric guitar?_
   Ashley _It's ninety-eight ninety-nine._   OR   _It's ninety-eight dollars and ninety-nine cents._
2. **Bryan** _____
   Ashley _____
3. **Bryan** _____
   Ashley _____
4. **Bryan** _____
   Ashley _____

C Complete the sentences with the words in the box.

☐ are ☐ him ☐ is ☐ it's ☐ them
☐ her ☐ how ☑ it ☐ much ☐ they're

1. Country music is boring. I don't like ___it___ at all.
2. _____ much _____ the wall calendars?
3. Beyoncé's my favorite singer. I like _____ a lot.
4. The science kits are very expensive. _____ $89.99 each!
5. How _____ _____ the star map?
6. The Rolling Stones are great. I really like _____!
7. Joss Stone is my favorite singer. I like _____ a lot.
8. This puzzle is cool. And _____ only $12.99.

2. Listening

Rick and Beverly talk about music at Beverly's birthday party. Listen and check (✓) the correct answers.

1. Beverly's favorite kind of music is _____.
   ☐ hip-hop   ☑ pop
2. Rick thinks Carrie Underwood _____.
   ☐ isn't interesting   ☐ is great
3. Beverly _____ country music.
   ☐ likes   ☐ doesn't like
4. Yo-Yo Ma is a _____ musician.
   ☐ jazz   ☐ classical
5. Rick and Beverly buy a lot of music _____.
   ☐ at the mall   ☐ online
6. On the Internet, one song is _____.
   ☐ $0.99   ☐ $99.00

Time for a Game?
See page 117.

Lesson 15: Our interests

1. Vocabulary

A These students sign up for a summer exchange program. Read about their free-time activities. Then listen and practice.

Lucas: I go camping.

Dana: I write poetry.

Karen: I go dancing a lot.

Fred: I spend time at the beach.

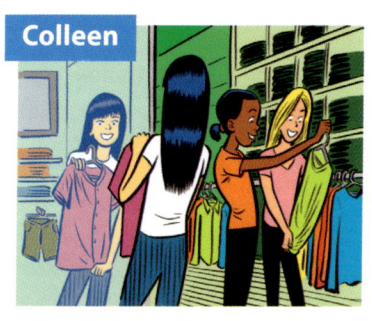

Colleen: I go shopping with my friends.

Kim: I do crossword puzzles.

B Match two students in Part A to the host student below with similar interests. Then write their names.

Celso, Brazil: I love the outdoors. I'm a very active person.

Kelly, Canada: I stay home a lot. I like quiet activities.

Marta, Puerto Rico: I go out, and I do a lot of things with my friends.

C You want to be a host student. How do you describe yourself? Tell your classmates. Use words from Part A or your own ideas.

I like sports. I play tennis a lot. I spend time with my friends. I . . .

2. Language focus

A Daniela applies to an exchange program. Read her application form. Then listen and practice.

T.65

> **like / don't like + to (verb)**
>
> I **like to go** shopping.
> I **like to play** video games.
> I **don't like to practice** the piano.

1. Name: _Daniela da Costa_   2. Age: _16_
3. Country: _Brazil_
4. Activities you like to do / don't like to do:
   I like to go swimming. I also like to go
   shopping. I don't like to watch TV.
5. Do you like to go camping? _No, I don't._
6. Do you like to spend time at home?
   Yes, I do.

B Complete the form with your own information.

1. Name: _____   2. Age: _____
3. Country: _____
4. Activities you like to do / don't like to do:
   _____
   _____
5. Do you like to go camping? _____
6. Do you like to spend time at home? _____

C Tell your classmates things you like and don't like to do. Use Exercise 1A or your own information.

> I like to listen to music. I don't like to go camping. I . . .

3. Listening

T.66

An exchange student, Karen, is staying with Marta's family. Marta is talking to her friend Eve about the experience. Who likes to do these activities? Listen and check (✓) the correct boxes.

	Karen	Marta	Karen and Marta
1. go dancing	☐	☐	☐
2. go shopping	☐	☐	☐
3. play tennis	☐	☐	☐
4. go to the movies	☐	☐	☐

My Interests

Lesson 16: In and out of school

1. Language focus

A Take the survey. Circle a letter to complete each sentence.

Adverbs of frequency

100%
- I **always** do my homework.
- I **usually** come to class on time.
- { **Sometimes** I talk in class.
- { I **sometimes** talk in class.
- I **hardly ever** sleep in class.

0%
- I **never** throw paper airplanes.

SURVEY
What Kind of Student Are You?

1. I _____ do my homework.
   a. always
   b. usually
   c. sometimes
   d. hardly ever
   e. never

2. I _____ come to class on time.
   a. always
   b. usually
   c. sometimes
   d. hardly ever
   e. never

3. I _____ listen to the teacher.
   a. always
   b. usually
   c. sometimes
   d. hardly ever
   e. never

4. I _____ answer a lot of the teacher's questions.
   a. always
   b. usually
   c. sometimes
   d. hardly ever
   e. never

5. I _____ listen to music on my headphones in class.
   a. always
   b. usually
   c. sometimes
   d. hardly ever
   e. never

6. I _____ get good grades.
   a. always
   b. usually
   c. sometimes
   d. hardly ever
   e. never

7. I _____ sleep in class.
   a. always
   b. usually
   c. sometimes
   d. hardly ever
   e. never

8. I _____ throw paper airplanes in class.
   a. always
   b. usually
   c. sometimes
   d. hardly ever
   e. never

B Zach completes the survey in Part A. Listen and write his answers on the lines. Then practice.

C Talk to four of your classmates. Find out their responses to the survey items.

You I always do my homework. How about you, Mario?
Classmate 1 I usually do my homework.
You I hardly ever sleep in class. How about you, Jen?
Classmate 2 I always answer a lot of the teacher's questions. How about you, . . . ?

2. Listening

A Ana talks about her weekend activities. How often does she do these things? Listen and write **A** (Ana) in the correct columns.

Weekend activities	Always	Usually	Sometimes	Hardly ever	Never
1. go dancing			A		
2. go shopping					
3. sleep late					
4. read books					
5. go bowling					

B How often does Charlie do the things in Part A? Listen again and write **C** (Charlie) in the correct columns in Part A.

3. Speaking

A What do you do after school? Write sentences. Use the activities in the box or your own ideas.

☐ do my homework   ☐ go shopping   ☐ play the guitar   ☐ use the Internet   ☐ watch TV

(always) *I always watch TV after school.*

1. (always) _____
2. (usually) _____
3. (sometimes) _____
4. (hardly ever) _____
5. (never) _____

B Work with a classmate. Read your sentences from Part A to each other. Then tell the class two things about your classmate.

> Nadia always goes to soccer practice after school. She hardly ever goes shopping.

My Interests

UNIT 4 Get Connected

Read

A Read the article quickly. Check (✓) the words you find.

☐ 1. boring ☐ 3. exciting ☐ 5. interesting
☐ 2. cool ☐ 4. fun ☐ 6. popular

Check Out Online Music Stores!

American teens like to listen to music. They spend a lot of time **downloading** songs from the Internet, and they usually listen to music on their cell phones. Where do they download songs from? From various online music stores. There are a few stores that are very large companies and sell all kinds of music on the Internet, and there are some other stores for specific audiences. And they are not only popular in the U.S. People from many countries now buy and download songs from these stores.

Some large companies have more than 20 **million** songs – from rock to classical to rap to country. And they also **sell** TV shows, movies, **podcasts**, and **e-books**. How much are songs? One song is usually $0.99 and an **album** is about $9.99. TV shows are around $2.99, and you can **rent** a new HD movie for $4.99.

You don't need to go to a music store or a bookstore. Check out any online music store. It's really **convenient** . . . and it's fun.

More Vocabulary Practice? See page 123.

B 🎧 T.70 Read the article slowly. Check your answers in Part A.

C Answer the questions.

1. Do American teens like to listen to music? *Yes, they do.*
2. Do American teens usually spend a lot of time downloading songs? _____
3. How many songs do large online music stores have? _____
4. How much is one song? _____
5. How much are new HD movies? _____

54 Unit 4

I always listen to country.

Listen

A 🎧 T.71 **Yuki and Carlos talk about music. Listen and answer the questions.**

1. Does Carlos often go to music stores? _No, he doesn't._
2. Does Yuki have an MP3 player? _____
3. Does Carlos like to listen to country music? _____
4. Does Yuki like to listen to country music? _____
5. Does Yuki often go to music stores on Mondays? _____

B What do you think? Write *I agree, I disagree,* or *I'm not sure.*

1. It's fun to listen to music on MP3 players. _____
2. Downloading music online is easy. _____
3. Music stores (not online) are convenient. _____
4. Country music is cool. _____
5. Rock music is exciting. _____

Your turn

Write

A Think about your musical habits. Answer the questions.

1. What kind of music do you like? _____
2. Do you usually listen to CDs? _____
3. Do you listen to music online? _____
4. Do you have an MP3 player? _____
5. How much time do you usually spend downloading songs?
   _____

B Write about your musical habits. Use the answers in Part A to help you.

I like _____ music a lot, and I like _____ music, too.

My Interests

UNIT 4 Review

Language chart review

her / him / it / them	like / don't like + to (verb)
She's cool. I like **her**.	I **like to hang out** with friends.
He's a pop singer. I like **him** a lot.	I **don't like to stay** home.
Jazz is boring. I don't like **it**.	
These CDs are great. I like **them**.	

A Read these sentences. Then write sentences with *like* or *don't like*.

1. My new neighbors are great!
   I like them.

2. That book is boring.
   _____

3. She's my best friend.
   _____

4. My baby brother is really cute.
   _____

5. Snakes are dangerous.
   _____

6. I think rock is cool.
   _____

B Josh writes an e-mail message to you. Read Josh's message. Then complete your message to him. Tell him about your free-time activities.

Hi!
My name's Josh. Here are some of the things I like to do: listen to music, go camping, spend time with my family, and play the piano.

But I don't dance. I don't play basketball or soccer. I'm musical, but I'm not athletic! How about you? What are your interests?

Your friend,
Josh

Dear Josh,
Hi! My name's _____.
Here are some of the things I like to do:
_____
_____
Here are some of the things I don't like to do:
_____
_____

Please write again soon.
Your friend, _____

56 Unit 4

Language chart review

How much is / are . . . ?	Adverbs of frequency
How much is this DVD? It's $29.99. How much are those boots? They're $60.00.	100% I **always** get good grades. I **usually** get up early. **Sometimes** I / I **sometimes** hang out with friends. I **hardly ever** go to bed early. 0% I **never** stay home on Friday night.

C Complete the questions with *How much is* or *How much are*. Then look at the photos, and answer the questions.

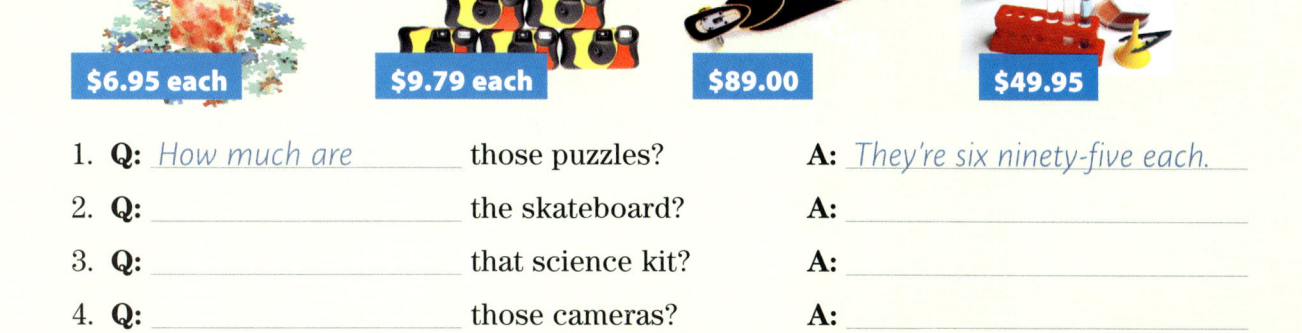

$6.95 each $9.79 each $89.00 $49.95

1. **Q:** _How much are_ those puzzles?   **A:** _They're six ninety-five each._
2. **Q:** _____ the skateboard?   **A:** _____
3. **Q:** _____ that science kit?   **A:** _____
4. **Q:** _____ those cameras?   **A:** _____

D How often does Sam do these things? Look at his schedule. Then write sentences with *always*, *usually*, *sometimes*, *hardly ever*, or *never*.

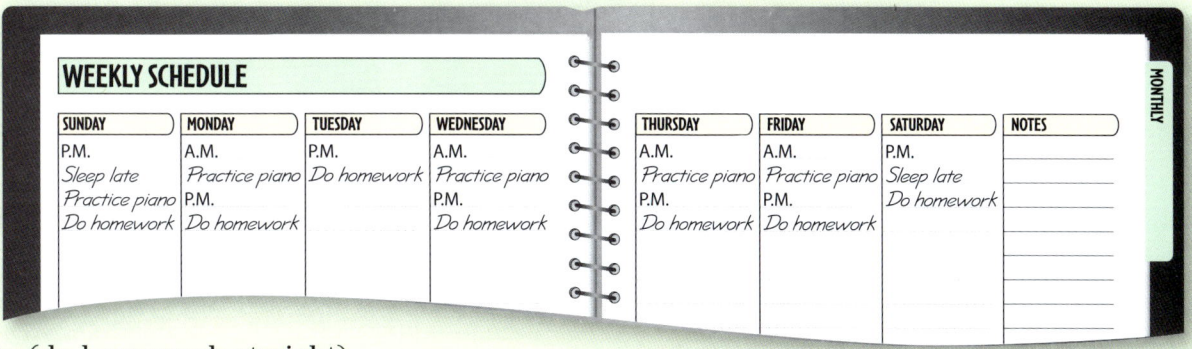

WEEKLY SCHEDULE

SUNDAY	MONDAY	TUESDAY	WEDNESDAY	THURSDAY	FRIDAY	SATURDAY	NOTES
P.M. Sleep late Practice piano Do homework	A.M. Practice piano P.M. Do homework	P.M. Do homework	A.M. Practice piano P.M. Do homework	A.M. Practice piano P.M. Do homework	A.M. Practice piano P.M. Do homework	P.M. Sleep late Do homework	

1. (do homework at night)

   I always do my homework at night.

2. (sleep late)

   _____

3. (practice the piano in the morning)

   _____

4. (practice the piano in the afternoon)

   _____

5. (go bowling)

Time for the Theme Project? See page 129.

Lesson 17: In San Francisco

1. Vocabulary

A Claudia and her family are on vacation in San Francisco. What do they do there? Match the photos to the correct activities. Then listen and practice.

Visit San Francisco

In San Francisco, they . . .

- ☐ buy souvenirs.
- ☐ ride a trolley.
- ☐ take a boat ride.
- ☐ *1* visit a museum.
- ☐ go sightseeing.
- ☐ see a show.
- ☐ take pictures.
- ☐ walk in the park.

B What can people do in your town or city? Write the activities. Use Part A or your own ideas.

1. *Take a boat ride.*
2. _____
3. _____
4. _____
5. _____
6. _____

UNIT 5 Favorite Activities

2. Language focus

A Claudia is videotaping her trip to San Francisco. Listen and practice.

Today is our first day in San Francisco. I'm videotaping our trip. Right now, we're visiting Fisherman's Wharf. Let's see . . . There are Mom and Dad. They're buying souvenirs. My cousin, Ruben, is eating lunch over there. My brother, Oscar, is taking pictures with his new camera. And now you see me. You can do so much in San Francisco. It's a great city!

> **Present continuous: affirmative statements**
>
> I**'m videotaping** our trip.
> She**'s taking** pictures.
> We**'re visiting** Fisherman's Wharf.
> You**'re skateboarding**.
> They**'re buying** souvenirs.
>
> buying = buy + ing
> taking = take + ing

B Everybody's doing different things now. Write the sentences with the correct forms of the verbs. Then listen and check.

1. (Ruben / go sightseeing) *He's going sightseeing.*
2. (Mom and Dad / see a show) _____
3. (Oscar / take pictures) _____
4. (Oscar and I / take a boat ride) _____

3. Speaking

A Work with two classmates. Imagine you are on vacation right now. Where are you? What are you doing?

You I'm in San Francisco. I'm visiting a museum.
Classmate 1 I'm at the beach. I'm swimming.
Classmate 2 I'm in Puerto Rico. I'm taking pictures.

B Tell the class about your classmates.

You Mario is at the beach. He's swimming.
Tori is in Puerto Rico. She's taking pictures.

Lesson 18: At the park

1. Vocabulary

A Ms. Nolan and Mr. Brown take their students to the park. Match the rules in the box to the correct signs in the picture. Then listen and practice.

1. Eat in the picnic area.
2. Sit down in the boat.
3. Stand in line.
4. Stay on the bike path.
5. Throw trash in the trash can.
6. Wait for the green light.

B Look at Part A again. Read the sentences and check (✓) T (true) or F (false).

			T	F
1.		They're waiting for the green light.	✓	☐
2.		Molly and Peter are staying on the bike path.	☐	☐
3.		The girls are eating in the picnic area.	☐	☐
4.		Dan is standing in line.	☐	☐
5.		He's throwing trash in the trash can.	☐	☐

2. Language focus

A The students aren't following the rules. Listen and practice.

Ms. Nolan	Oh, no. The students aren't following the rules! Look at Dan. He isn't standing in line.
Mr. Brown	Hey, Dan! You aren't standing in line!
Ms. Nolan	And look at Molly and Peter. They aren't staying on the bike path.
Mr. Brown	Molly! Peter! Please stay on the bike path.
Ms. Nolan	Oh, no, wait! It's a red light. I'm not paying attention.
Mr. Brown	You're right. Now *we* aren't following the rules!

Present continuous: negative statements

I'm not paying attention.
You aren't standing in line.
He isn't standing in line.
We aren't following the rules.
They aren't staying on the bike path.

aren't = are not   isn't = is not

B Look at the picture in Exercise 1A again. What are the students doing wrong? Complete the sentences. Then listen and check.

1. Dan *isn't standing in line* .
2. Molly and Peter _____ .
3. Fred _____ .
4. Brad and Jeff _____ .
5. Lisa _____ .
6. Nan _____ .

3. Listening

Now what are the students doing wrong? Listen and match the two parts of each sentence.

1. Nan and Lisa aren't *b*
2. Jeff isn't ___
3. Dan and Fred aren't ___
4. Brad isn't ___
5. Molly isn't ___

a. sitting down in the boat.
b. eating in the picnic area.
c. standing in line.
d. staying on the bike path.
e. throwing trash in the trash can.

In San Francisco

Lessons 17 & 18 Mini-review

1. Language check

A Write the present continuous form of the verbs.

1. sit _sitting_
2. skate _____
3. wait _____
4. throw _____
5. pay _____
6. stay _____
7. ride _____
8. swim _____
9. go _____

B Helena and her family are on vacation in New York City. Complete Helena's message to her friend Jane.

Dear Jane,

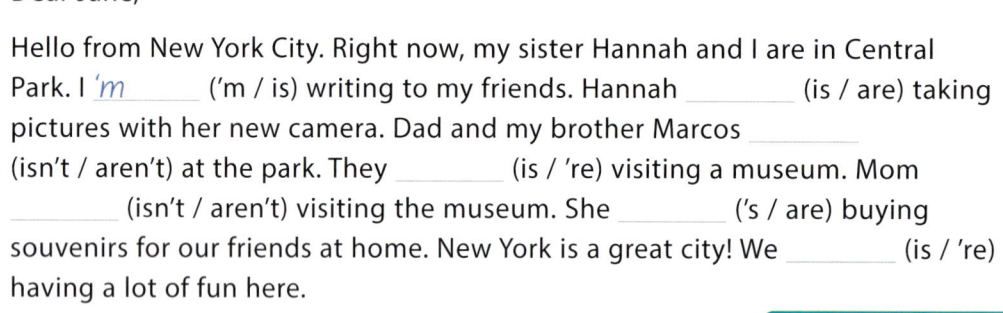

Hello from New York City. Right now, my sister Hannah and I are in Central Park. I _'m_ ('m / is) writing to my friends. Hannah _____ (is / are) taking pictures with her new camera. Dad and my brother Marcos _____ (isn't / aren't) at the park. They _____ (is / 're) visiting a museum. Mom _____ (isn't / aren't) visiting the museum. She _____ ('s / are) buying souvenirs for our friends at home. New York is a great city! We _____ (is / 're) having a lot of fun here.

See you soon!

Helena

C Use the cues to write sentences: ✓ = yes, ✗ = no.

1. Joe / wait for the green light (✓)
   Joe is waiting for the green light.

2. Alicia / sit down in the boat (✗)
   _____

3. Dmitri / stand in line (✗)
   _____

4. Ginny / eat in the picnic area (✓)
   _____

5. Laura / stay on the bike path (✗)
   _____

6. Tony / throw trash in the trash can (✗)
   _____

D Look at the photos. What's everyone doing? Correct the sentences.

7:00 a.m.

1. Kate's reading a book. *She isn't reading a book. She's doing her homework.*
2. Rafael's taking a boat ride. _____
3. Claudia's visiting a museum. _____
4. Zach's watching a video. _____

7:00 p.m.

5. Rafael's walking in the park. _____
6. Zach's taking pictures. _____
7. Kate's standing in line. _____
8. Claudia's eating lunch. _____

2. Listening

Kate is busy today. Where is she? Listen and number the sentences from 1 to 4.

She's in the park. _____   She's at the movie theater. _____

She's in a store. _____   She's in school. _____

Time for a Game?
See page 118.

In San Francisco **63**

Lesson 19: At the beach

1. Vocabulary

A What are these people doing at the beach? Match the two parts of each sentence. Then listen and practice.

1. Two boys are _h_
2. A baby is ____
3. Two girls are ____
4. A family is ____
5. A dog is ____
6. A man is ____
7. A boy is ____
8. A girl is ____

a. collecting seashells.
b. floating on a raft.
c. flying a kite.
d. having a picnic.
e. playing in the sand.
f. sailing a boat.
g. swimming in the ocean.
h. throwing a Frisbee.

B What do you do at the beach? Write sentences about two things you do and two things you don't do.

Things I do at the beach	Things I don't do at the beach
I swim in the ocean.	I don't collect seashells.

2. Language focus

Present continuous: Yes / No questions

Is she **playing** in the sand?
 Yes, she **is**.
 No, she **isn't**.
Are they **throwing** a Frisbee?
 Yes, they **are**.
 No, they **aren't**.

A Marty and Ella look for each other at the beach. Listen and practice.

Ella Hi, Marty. It's Ella. I'm at the beach. Where are you?
Marty Hi, Ella. I'm at the beach, too.
Ella Really? I'm sitting near a lifeguard chair.
Marty Hmm. Me, too. I don't see you, but I see a little girl in a red bathing suit.
Ella Me, too. Is she playing in the sand?
Marty No, she isn't. She's collecting seashells.
Ella Seashells? I guess there are a lot of girls in red bathing suits here today!

B Complete the rest of the conversation. Listen and check. Then practice.

Ella OK, are you sitting near two boys?
Marty Yes, I ___am___ .
Ella _____ they _____ a Frisbee?
Marty No, they _____ . They're eating lunch on the beach.
Ella Hmm. _____ a boy _____ a kite?
Marty Um, no. Do you see two girls near the ocean?
Ella Yes, I do.
Marty _____ they _____ seashells?
Ella _____ , they aren't. They're having a picnic. Hey! _____ we talking about the same beach?

3. Listening

Lee calls Hannah from the beach. Are these sentences true or false? Listen and check (✓) T (true) or F (false).

	T	F
1. Naomi is swimming in the ocean.	✓	
2. Tom and Ken are playing ball.		
3. Dave is sailing a boat.		
4. Megan is floating on a raft.		
5. Lee is taking a boat ride.		
6. Hannah is doing homework now.		

Lesson 20 — At the store

1. Vocabulary

A Ana, Clara, Rafael, Zach, and Tommy are at the store. Listen and practice.

1. Ana and Clara are shopping for jewelry.
2. Rafael is trying on a jacket. 
3. Zach is paying for a baseball glove. 
4. Tommy is looking at comic books. 

B Look at the items for sale at the store. Listen and practice.

1. a bracelet
2. a coat 
3. a tennis racket 
4. a surfboard 
5. a ring 
6. a scarf 
7. a necklace 
8. a belt 
9. a baseball bat 

C Write the name of each item from Part B in the correct column.

Jewelry	Clothes	Sports equipment
bracelet		

66   Unit 5

2. Language focus

A Ana sees Zach at the store.
Listen and practice.

> **Zach** Hi, Ana. What are you doing?
> **Ana** I'm here with Clara. We're shopping for jewelry. How about you?
> **Zach** Oh, I'm just looking at everything here.
> **Ana** Rafael and Tommy are here, too.
> **Zach** Really? What are they doing?
> **Ana** Well, Tommy's looking at comic books, and Rafael's trying on clothes.
> **Zach** Oh. What's he trying on?
> **Ana** He's trying on a jacket. It's red and black. It's really cool.
> **Zach** I have a red and black jacket, too. Hey, Rafael! That's my jacket!

Present continuous: *What* questions

What are you doing?
　I'm looking at everything.
What are you doing?
　We're shopping for jewelry.
What's he trying on?
　He's trying on a jacket.
What are they doing?
　They're looking at comic books.

B The friends continue to shop. Write questions. Listen and check. Then practice.

1. **Tommy** *What's Ana trying on?* (Ana / try on)
   Rafael She's trying on a bracelet.
2. **Rafael** _____ (you / look at)
   Ana We're looking at some jewelry.
3. **Ana** _____ (you / do)
   Zach I'm shopping for a surfboard.
4. **Clara** _____ (Rafael / pay for)
   Tommy He's paying for a belt.
5. **Zach** _____ (Ana and Clara / try on)
   Tommy They're trying on some clothes.

3. Pronunciation Stress

Listen. Notice the stress. Then listen again and practice.

What are you **doing**?
What are you **looking** for?
What's he trying **on**?
What's she **buying**?

4. Speaking

Work with a classmate. Name two of your family members. Then ask and answer questions about what they are doing now. Use the correct stress in the questions.

I have a sister.　　What's she doing now?　　She's studying.

In San Francisco 67

UNIT 5 Get Connected

Read

A Read the letter quickly. Are these statements true or false? Write *True* or *False*.

1. It's Paulo's third trip to Japan. _____
2. Okayama is a really beautiful city. _____
3. The apples in Okayama are delicious. _____

Our Trip So Far

Dear Rodrigo,

Today is my family's third day in Japan, and we're really enjoying our trip. Right now, I'm sitting in a park and writing about our trip so far. Today, we're in Okayama. There are many interesting things here – museums, a **castle**, parks, shops, and restaurants. It's a really beautiful city.

We're near the castle right now. My mother is looking at everything and taking pictures. Oh, and my father's buying souvenirs – some postcards and some books. My sister's with him. She's standing in line, but she isn't buying souvenirs. She's buying **tickets** for a show tonight – a **traditional** Japanese **play**. Cool!

In the shop next to me, people are buying Momotaro ("**Peach** Boy") **dolls**. Momotaro is an important boy in some old Japanese stories. He's from Okayama. And the peaches in Okayama are famous. They're **delicious**. I'm eating one now. Talk to you later!

Bye-bye,

Paulo

More Vocabulary Practice? See page 124.

B 🎧 T.89 Read the letter slowly. Check your answers in Part A.

C Answer the questions.

1. Is Paulo's family enjoying their trip? *Yes, they are.*
2. What's Paulo doing? _____
3. Is his mother taking pictures? _____
4. Is his father buying tickets for a play? _____
5. What's his sister doing? _____

I'm really bored.

Listen

A Luisa and Matt talk about a vacation. Listen and answer the questions.

1. Is Matt enjoying the trip? *No, he isn't.*
2. What's Matt doing? _____
3. Is Matt's father collecting seashells? _____
4. Is Timmy swimming in the ocean? _____
5. What are Matt's mom and sister buying? _____
6. What are Matt's grandparents doing? _____

B What do you think? Answer the questions.

1. Do you think family trips are fun? _____
2. Do you think a beach trip is exciting? _____
3. Do you think traditional shows are interesting? _____
4. Do you think souvenirs are fun gifts? _____

Your turn

Write

A Imagine you and your family are sightseeing on a trip. Answer the questions.

1. Where are you? _____
2. What's the place like? _____
3. Where are you sitting and writing the message? _____
4. What are your family members doing? _____
5. Are you and your family enjoying the trip? _____

B Write a message to your friend about your trip. Use the answers in Part A to help you.

In San Francisco

UNIT 5 Review

Language chart review

Present continuous statements	
Affirmative	**Negative**
I'**m buying** a bracelet. You'**re standing** in line. She'**s walking** in the park. We'**re having** a picnic. They'**re visiting** a museum.	I'**m not looking at** souvenirs. You **aren't eating** lunch. She **isn't sleeping**. We **aren't sitting** at the beach. They **aren't taking** a boat ride.

A Complete the stories. Be sure to use the correct forms of the verbs and verb phrases.

Story 1

Hi! I'm Rachel. *I'm not going to school* (I / not / go to school) today. _____ (I / hang out) with my friend, Lissa, today. _____ (we / go sightseeing) in the city. Right now, _____ (we / visit) a museum. _____ (Lissa / buy) souvenirs, and _____ (I / stand) in line. I'm really thirsty, so _____ (I / have) a soda. _____ (Lissa / eat) an ice-cream cone while we wait to go into the museum.

Story 2

Some people _____ (see) a show, but one man _____ (not / listen) to the actors. He _____ (not / follow) the theater's rules. He _____ (not / throw) his trash in the trash can. Another man _____ (not / watch) the show. He's asleep!

70 Unit 5

Language chart review

Present continuous Yes / No and What questions

Are you **listening** to music? Yes, I **am**. / No, I'**m not**.	**What** are you **listening to**? I'**m listening to** my new CD.
Is he **walking** in the park? Yes, he **is**. / No, he **isn't**.	**What's** he **doing**? He'**s walking in** the park.
Are they **trying on** clothes? Yes, they **are**. / No, they **aren't**.	**What** are they **trying on**? They'**re trying on** coats.

B Look again at Part A. Write questions and answers.

1. Rachel and Lissa / visit a museum today
   Q: *Are Rachel and Lissa visiting a museum today?*   A: *Yes, they are.*
2. Lissa / stand in line
   Q: _____   A: _____
3. Rachel / wear jeans
   Q: _____   A: _____
4. the people / see a show
   Q: _____   A: _____
5. the man / talk on the phone
   Q: _____   A: _____

C Write questions to complete the conversations.

1. **A** *What are your friends doing?*
   B My friends? They're throwing a Frisbee in the yard.
2. **A** _____
   B No, we aren't eating. We're doing homework.
3. **A** _____
   B He's wearing jeans.
4. **A** _____
   B My mom's painting the kitchen.
5. **A** _____
   B I'm eating a sandwich. I'm hungry!
6. **A** _____
   B They're listening to rock music.

Time for the Theme Project? See page 130.

Lesson 21: Where are you going?

1. Vocabulary

A Look at these events. Complete the sentences with the words in the box. Then listen and practice.

- ✓ **amazing** robots
- ☐ **fascinating** animals
- ☐ **popular** movies
- ☐ **awesome** musicians
- ☐ **incredible** teams
- ☐ **thrilling** shows

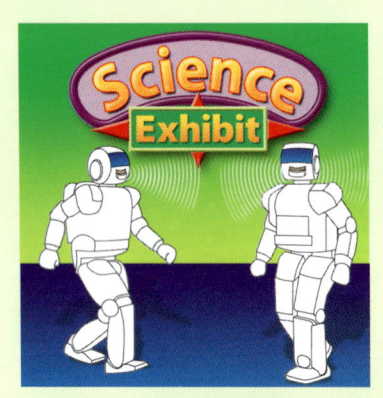

1. _Amazing robots_ walk and talk!
2. These _____ are fun for children and adults! 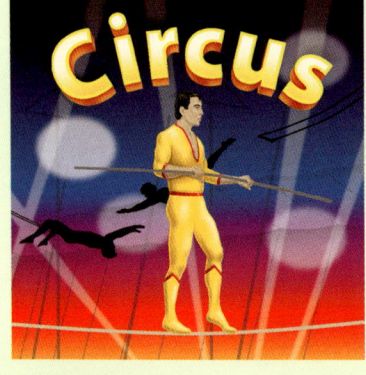
3. Learn about these _____ 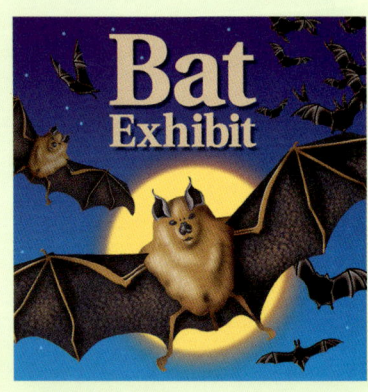
4. See six _____ for only $18.00.
5. Two _____ play on Saturday. 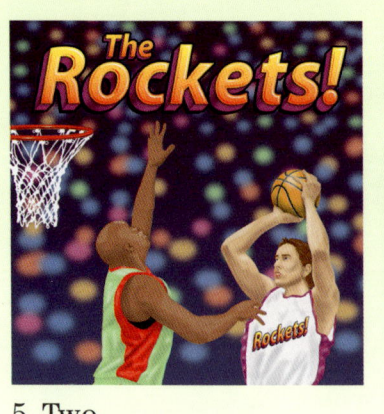
6. _____ play rock and country music! 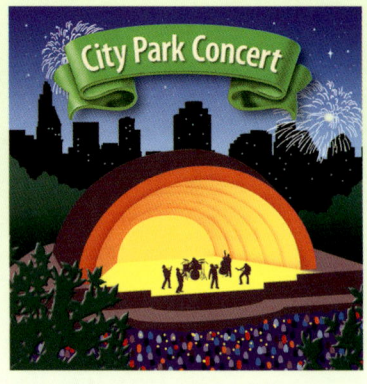

B Complete the sentences with your opinions. Then tell a classmate.

1. _Cristiano Ronaldo_ is an incredible athlete.
2. _____ is a thrilling movie.
3. _____ are amazing animals.
4. _____ is an awesome singer.
5. _____ is a fascinating class.
6. _____ is a popular song.

> Cristiano Ronaldo is an incredible athlete.

UNIT 6 Entertainment

2. Language focus

A Claudia and her little brother, Oscar, meet Rafael. They talk about where they're going. Listen and practice.

> **Where + (be) ... going?**
>
> **Where are** you **going**?
> I**'m going** to the basketball game.
> We**'re going** to the Nature Center.

Rafael Claudia! Oscar!
Claudia Rafael? What a surprise! Where are you going?
Rafael I'm going to the basketball game. I want to see the Rockets. They're an incredible team!
Claudia Yeah, I know! They're awesome!
Rafael How about you two? Where are you going?
Claudia We're going to the Nature Center.
Oscar There's a bat exhibit today!
Rafael Really? Do you like bats?
Claudia I hate bats, but Oscar thinks they're fascinating.

B Where are these people going? Write questions and answers. Listen and check. Then practice.

1. **Q:** *Where's he going?*
   A: *He's going to the movies.*
2. **Q:**
   A:
3. **Q:**
   A:
4. **Q:**
   A:
5. **Q:**
   A:
6. **Q:**
   A:

3. Listening

Where are these people going? Listen and check (✓) the correct information.

1. Joanne ☐ to a concert ☐ to her piano lesson
2. Jerome ☐ home ☐ to soccer practice
3. Cynthia ☐ to the library ☐ to Sarah's house
4. Ruben ☐ to the circus ☐ to the beach

Lesson 22: Birthday parties

1. Vocabulary

A What do these people like to do on their birthdays?
Complete the sentences with the verb phrases in the box.
Then listen and practice.

- ☐ celebrate at a restaurant
- ☐ have a barbecue
- ☐ play cards
- ☐ relax at home
- ☑ eat cake
- ☐ open presents
- ☐ play party games
- ☐ sing songs

1. Sarah likes to _eat cake_.
2. Tim likes to _____. 
3. Diana likes to _____. 
4. Greg likes to _____. 
5. Paul likes to _____. 
6. Jack likes to _____. 
7. Rita likes to _____. 
8. Hilary likes to _____. 

B Work with two classmates. Talk about what you like to do on your birthdays.

You What do you like to do on your birthday, Nellie?
Classmate 1 I like to open my presents! How about you?
Classmate 2 I like to . . .

74 Unit 6

2. Language focus

Simple present vs. present continuous
My mom usually **cooks**.
My dad **is cooking** hot dogs now.

A It's Rita's birthday. How is her family celebrating? Listen and practice.

We usually eat in the kitchen, but not today. My mom usually cooks. But my dad is cooking hot dogs now. He always cooks on my birthday.

We usually eat at 6:00. But it's 7:30 now, and we're still waiting for our dinner. My dad is a good cook. But he's very slow!

B Rita's family is relaxing after the barbecue. What are they doing now? What do they usually do after dinner? Write sentences. Then listen and check.

NOW — 8:00 p.m.
USUALLY — 8:00 p.m.

1. Rita _is playing cards_ . _She usually practices the violin._
2. Mr. Cookson _____ . _____
3. Mrs. Cookson _____ . _____
4. Peter _____ . _____
5. Lucy _____ . _____

3. Listening

Tommy's aunt calls on his birthday. Does Tommy talk about what people in his family usually do or about what they are doing now? Listen and check (✓) the correct column.

	Usually	Now
1. Tommy's brother	☐	☐
2. Tommy's little sister	☐	☐
3. Tommy's mother	☐	☐
4. Tommy's father	☐	☐

Entertainment 75

Lessons 21 & 22 Mini-review

1. Language check

A The sports announcers are at an ice-skating event. Complete their sentences with the correct forms of the verbs.

1. Look! Here's Terry. _He's skating_ (he / skate) across the rink.
2. ___ always ___ (he / skate) so beautifully.
3. And now ___ (he / dance) on the ice.
4. Oh! Look! ___ (he / jump)! Amazing!
5. Of course, ___ (he / practice) every day.
6. OK. Now ___ (he / wait) for his scores.

B The competition is finished. What are these people doing now? What do they usually do at night? Write sentences.

1. The announcers: _They're eating dinner at a restaurant._   _They usually stay home._
   (eat dinner at a restaurant)   (stay home)
2. Terry: ___   ___
   (talk to fans)   (watch TV)
3. Diana, the coach: ___   ___
   (sleep)   (read sports magazines)

C Choose the correct words to complete the conversations.

1. **Jack** Hi, Sarah. ___Where___ (What / Where) are you?
   Sarah _____ (I'm / She's) on the bus.
   Jack On the bus? Where _____ (is / are) you going?
   Sarah I'm with Joanna. _____ (He's / We're) going to the mall.
   Jack But today's Monday. What about school?
   Sarah Well, we usually _____ (go / are going) to school on Monday, but today's a holiday.
   Jack Oh, yeah, that's right. Well, have fun!

2. **Greg** Hi, Paul. Where _____ (are / is) you going today?
   Paul _____ (I'm / She's) going to the park.
   Greg Really? You usually _____ (work / is working) on Saturday.
   Paul I know, but there's a concert today.
   Greg Cool! Well, have a good time.
   Paul Thanks. Oh . . . the concert _____ (starts / is starting) now. Talk to you later.

2. Listening

Mariah is talking about her birthday party. What does she usually do? What's she doing now? Listen and check (✓) Usually or Now.

T.99

	Usually	Now
1. have a party at home	☐	✓
2. celebrate at a restaurant	☐	☐
3. eat cake at a restaurant	☐	☐
4. relax at home	☐	☐
5. have a barbecue	☐	☐
6. sing songs	☐	☐

Time for a Game? See page 119.

Lesson 23

Let's see a movie.

1. Vocabulary

A Label the movies with the words in the box. Then listen and practice.

☐ an action movie ☑ a comedy ☐ a drama
☐ an animated movie ☐ a documentary ☐ a horror movie

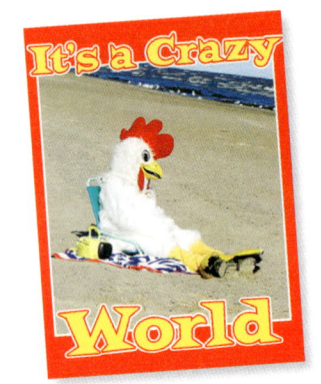

1. This is _a comedy_.
2. This is _____. 
3. This is _____. 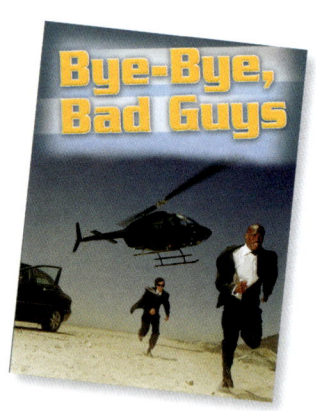
4. This is _____. 
5. This is _____. 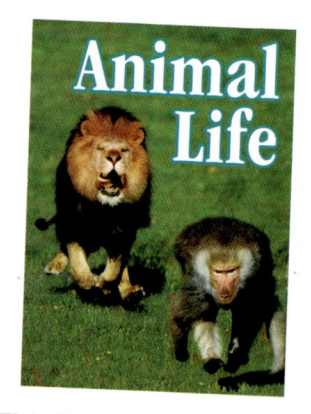
6. This is _____. 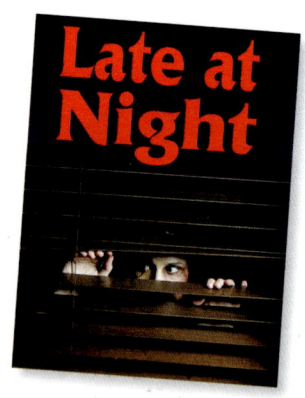

B Write the plural form of each kind of movie. Then write your opinion using *like* or *don't like*.

Singular	Plural	Your opinion
1. a comedy	comedies	I like comedies.
2. a horror movie		
3. an action movie		
4. a drama		
5. a documentary		
6. an animated movie		

2. Language focus

want / don't want + to (verb)
I **want to go** to the movies tonight.
I **don't want to see** a horror movie.
Do you **want to come**?
  Yes, I **do**. / No, I **don't**.
What **do** you **want to see**?
  I **want to see** a horror movie.

A Rafael invites Ana to a movie. Listen and practice.
T.101

Rafael   I want to go to the movies tonight. Do you want to come?
Ana   Well, what do you want to see?
Rafael   I want to see a horror movie – *Late at Night*. It's a new movie. It's very popular. Julia James is in it. She's awesome!
Ana   Well, thanks, but I don't want to see a horror movie. I want to stay home and watch TV.

B Now Rafael invites Kate. Complete the conversation. Listen and check. Then practice.
T.102

Rafael   _Do_ you _want to_ go to the movies?
Kate   No. I _____ to go to the movies.
Rafael   Are you sure? I want to see *Late at Night*.
Kate   Sorry. I really _____ go.
Rafael   OK. _____ you _____ a drama on TV?
Kate   No. I don't like dramas.
Rafael   Well, what _____ you _____ do?
Kate   I _____ stay home and sleep.

3. Pronunciation   Reduction

Listen. Notice how *want to* is reduced in conversation. Then listen again and practice.
T.103

| I **wanna** see an action movie. | They **wanna** go to the concert. |
| We **wanna** have a picnic. | I **wanna** play video games. |

4. Listening

What does each person want to see? Listen and check (✓) the correct kind of movie.
T.104

	A comedy	A horror movie	An action movie	A drama	A documentary	An animated movie
1. Ted	✓	☐	☐	☐	☐	☐
2. Joe	☐	☐	☐	☐	☐	☐
3. Maggie	☐	☐	☐	☐	☐	☐
4. Connie	☐	☐	☐	☐	☐	☐

Entertainment

Lesson 24

In line at the movies

1. Vocabulary

A Read the descriptions and look at the people waiting in line at the movies. Match the people to the correct sentences. Then listen and practice.

Carlos is tall and slim. He has wavy, black hair. ____
Carolyn is short and heavy. She has short, straight, red hair. ____
David is short and slim. He has curly, black hair and blue eyes. ____
Kevin is average height. He has short, brown hair. ____
Marci is average height. She has medium-length hair and brown eyes. ____
Sandra is tall and slim. She has long, blond hair. _1_

B Complete the chart. Use the words from Part A.

Height	Body type	Hair length	Hairstyle	Hair color	Eye color
tall	slim	long	curly	blond	blue

80 Unit 6

2. Language focus

A Marci and Sandra are still in line at the movies. They're waiting for Sandra's friend, John. Listen and practice.

Sandra Where's John? I don't see him. The movie starts at 2:20!
Marci What does John look like?
Sandra He's tall and slim.
Marci What color is his hair?
Sandra It's blond. He has short, curly hair.
Marci I think I see him. He's near the end of the line. He's talking to a girl.
Sandra What does the girl look like?
Marci She has long, brown hair, and she's wearing a yellow blouse. Do you see her? She's cute.
Sandra Yes, I see her. I see John, too! He's not looking for *us*. I guess he's too busy!

What questions about people

What does John look like?
   He's tall and slim.
   He has short, curly hair.
   He has brown eyes.
What's his hair like?
   It's short and curly.
What color is his hair?
   It's blond.
What color are his eyes?
   They're blue.

B Look at the picture of Carolyn in Exercise 1A. Write a question for each answer. Then listen and check.

1. *What does she look like?* _____ She's short and heavy.
2. _____ It's short and straight.
3. _____ It's red.
4. _____ They're brown.

C Complete the questions with names of your classmates. Then write answers.

1. (boy) What does _____ look like? _____
2. (boy) What color is _____'s hair? _____
3. (girl) What's _____'s hair like? _____
4. (girl) What color are _____'s eyes? _____

3. Speaking

Play a game. Think of a teacher in your school. Your classmates ask questions and guess.

Classmate 1 Is it a man or a woman?
You It's a man.
Classmate 2 What color is his hair?
You It's blond.
Classmate 3 Is it curly?
You No. It's short and straight.
Classmate 4 Is it Mr. Santos?
You Yes, it is!

UNIT 6 Get Connected

Read

A Read the article quickly. Check (✓) the things you can do at the fair.

- ✓ eat great food
- ☐ listen to music
- ☐ see a movie
- ☐ have a barbecue
- ☐ play party games
- ☐ see thrilling talent shows

Come to the Fair!

It's August in Des Moines, Iowa. What are people doing? They're going to the famous Iowa State Fair. Every year in August, people from around the world go to this fair. For 11 days, people eat great food, listen to incredible music, and see thrilling talent shows and fascinating **farm** animals. But there's one thing that *everyone* wants to see at the fair: the **butter cow**!

The butter cow is a very popular exhibit. Every year someone – these days, Sarah Pratt – makes the butter cow. She uses a lot of butter and **wire**. It usually takes about 24 hours to make it. The cow is tall and very big. It **weighs** 600 **pounds**. And, of course, it's yellow! Both young and old people love to watch Sarah make it. You can't eat the butter cow, but it's amazing to look at it!

More Vocabulary Practice?
See page 124.

B T.108 Read the article slowly. Check your answers in Part A.

C Answer the questions.

1. Where do people come from to go to the Iowa State Fair?
   They come from around the world.

2. What do people usually do at the fair? Write two things.

3. What does everyone at the fair want to see?

4. Who makes the butter cow these days?

5. What's the butter cow like?

Forget the bookstore!

Listen

A 🎧 T.109   **Jean and Chris are talking about the town fair. Listen and answer the questions.**

1. Where's Chris going? <u>He's going to the bookstore.</u>
2. Where's Jean going? _____
3. What's the fair like? _____
4. Are the bands at the fair famous? _____
5. Does Chris want to go to the fair? _____

B **What do you think? Write *I agree*, *I disagree*, or *I'm not sure*.**

1. Fairs are fun. _____
2. Free concerts are a good idea. _____
3. The music of every famous band is great. _____
4. It's good to do things with friends. _____

Your turn

Write

A Imagine your ideal fair or festival. Answer the questions.

1. What's the name of the fair or festival? _____
2. When is it? _____
3. Where is it? _____
4. What fun things are there to do? _____
5. What can you eat there? _____
6. Who do you want to go with? _____

B Write about your ideal fair or festival. Use the answers in Part A to help you.

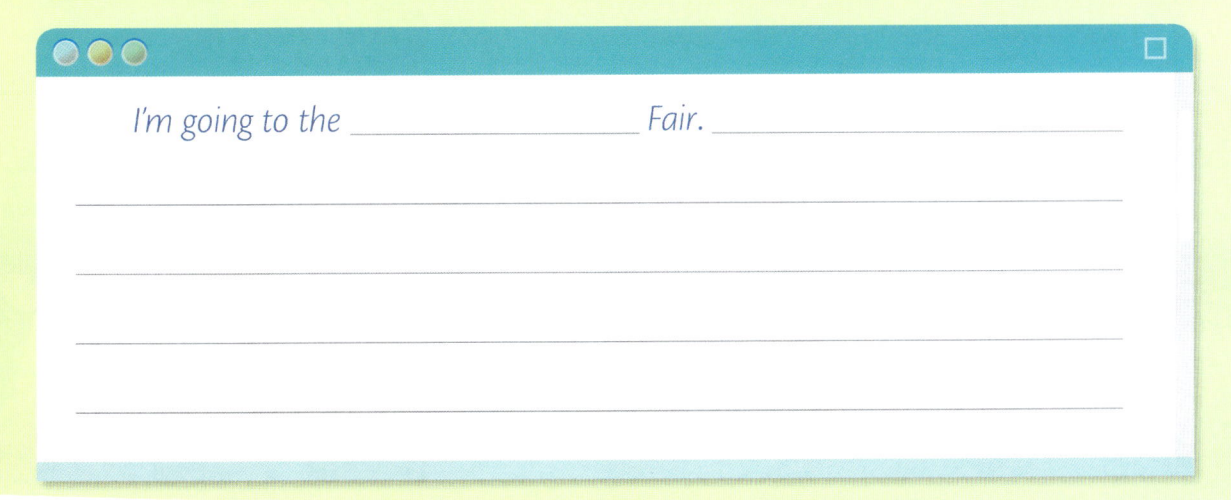

I'm going to the _____ *Fair.* _____

_____

_____

_____

Entertainment 83

UNIT 6 Review

Language chart review

Where + (be) . . . going?	want / don't want + to (verb)
Where are you **going**? I**'m going** to the circus. We**'re going** home. **Where's** Sarah **going**? She**'s going** to the concert.	**Do** you **want to come** to my house? Yes, I **do**. / No, I **don't**. What **do** you **want to do**? I **want to stay** home tonight. I **don't want to go** out.

A Blake Winters from *Connect! TV News* talks to people for a report called "Where Are You Going?" Complete the conversations with the correct forms of the verbs.

1. **Blake** Hi! *Where are you going?*
   (where / you / go?)

   Hugo _____
   (I / go / to my karate class.)

   Blake _____
   (where / your friend / go?)

   Hugo _____
   (she / go / to the mall.)

   May Yeah, I want to find some new sneakers.

   Blake Awesome!

2. **Blake** And _____
   (where / you / go?)

   Lori _____
   (we / go / to the movies.)

   Blake _____
   (what / you / want / to see?)

   Lori We want to see the new James Bond movie.
   Hey, Blake! _____
   (you / want / to come / with us?)

   Blake No, thanks. But have fun!

84 Unit 6

Language chart review

Simple present vs. present continuous	What questions about people	
I usually **practice** the piano after school. Today, I**'m reading** a book. We usually **sing** songs in music class. Today, we**'re listening** to CDs.	**What does Claire look like?** She**'s** short and slim. She **has** long, brown hair. **What's her hair like?** It**'s** long and straight.	**What color is her hair?** It**'s** black. **What color are her eyes?** They**'re** brown.

B Complete the sentences. Use the correct forms of the words in the box.

```
eat   play   talk   wear
```

1. My name's Eddie. I usually _wear_ jeans, but today I'm _wearing_ nice clothes. I always _____ nice clothes on my birthday.

2. Ramon is usually very shy. He hardly ever _____ in class, but today he's _____ a lot.

3. I'm Grace, and this is my family. We usually _____ dinner at home, but today is special. We're _____ in a restaurant. The cake at this restaurant is great!

4. Paula is _____ cards with Tony right now. They usually _____ cards on Sunday, but this week they're _____ on Saturday.

C Complete the conversations.

1. **Joe** My cousin wants to visit me. She wants to come in December.
   Lee Cool! What _does_ she _look_ like?
   Joe _____ pretty. _____ tall and slim. She _____ short, red _____ .
   Lee _____ color _____ her eyes?
   Joe _____ blue.

2. **Cara** There's a new boy in my class.
   Dora Really? What _____ he look _____ ?
   Cara _____ cute. He's short _____ heavy.
   Dora _____ his hair like?
   Cara He _____ curly, brown hair. Oh, and _____ eyes _____ brown.

3. **Val** I think my brother is in your English class.
   Dina Really? What _____ he _____ like?
   Val _____ tall and slim.
   Dina A lot of boys in the class are tall and slim!
   Val He _____ black hair, and _____ eyes _____ brown.
   Dina Oh, I know him!

Time for the Theme Project?
See page 131.

Entertainment 85

Lesson 25 — I'm hungry!

1. Vocabulary

A Match the items in the kitchen to the correct words. Then listen and practice. (T.110)

apples ___	broccoli ___	cheese ___	meat ___	rice _1_
bananas ___	butter ___	eggs ___	potatoes ___	water ___

B How often do you eat or drink the items in Part A at lunchtime? Write the items in the correct columns. Then tell your classmates.

Always	Sometimes	Never
	rice	

I sometimes eat rice.

UNIT 7 What We Eat

2. Language focus

A Zach is hungry. Listen and practice.

Zach Hey, Mom! I'm hungry, but there's nothing to eat.
Mom Nothing to eat? Look in the refrigerator. There's cheese . . .
Zach Yuck! I don't like cheese. Do we have ice cream?
Mom No, but we have bananas and apples, and . . .
Zach Mom, you know I don't like bananas!
Mom What about eggs? There's an egg. You can make an egg sandwich.
Zach No, thanks. I want a hot dog or a cookie.
Mom Oh, Zach. How about some healthy food for a change?

Countable and uncountable nouns

Countable nouns (things you can count)
Specific: There's **an egg** in the refrigerator.
General: I like egg**s**.

Uncountable nouns (things you cannot count)
Specific: There's **cheese** in the refrigerator.
General: I don't like **cheese**.

B Look at the items in the kitchen in Exercise 1A. Write the items in the correct columns. Then listen and check.

Countable nouns	Uncountable nouns
apples	

3. Speaking

Learn what foods four of your classmates like and don't like.

You I like carrots. I don't like broccoli. How about you, Kim?
Classmate 1 Well, I like pizza. I don't like meat. How about you, Freddie?
Classmate 2 Hmm. I like apples. I don't like eggs.
Classmate 3 Well, I like rice. I don't like bananas. How about you, Luis?
Classmate 4 I like cheese. I don't like . . .

Lesson 26

Picnic plans

1. Vocabulary

A Ana and Rafael plan a picnic. Listen and practice.

T.113

1. milk
2. cups
3. juice
4. bread
5. plates
6. fruit
7. pasta
8. spoons
9. forks
10. knives

B Where do the items in Part A belong? Write the items in the correct columns.

Food	Drinks	Supplies
		cups

88   Unit 7

2. Language focus

A The friends decide what they need for their picnic. Listen and practice.

Rafael OK, what do we need for the picnic? Um, how many cups do we have?
Ana Let's see. We have about 20 cups. But there are only 3 plates. We need plates.
Rafael OK. What about food? How much pasta is there?
Ana Um, there's a little pasta. We need pasta and a lot of milk. There's a little bread, but let's buy bread, too.
Rafael What else? How much juice do we have?
Ana I think we have a lot of juice.
Rafael Wait! Look at Zach! We need juice *now*!

How much / How many...?
Countable nouns
How many cups do we have? We have **20** cups. We have **a lot of** cups. There are **3** plates. There are **a few** plates.
Uncountable nouns
How much pasta is there? There's **a lot of** pasta. There's **a little** pasta.

B Look at the photos. Complete the questions and answers. Listen and check. Then practice.

1. **Q:** How many spoons are there?
   A: There are 4 spoons.

2. **Q:** _____
   A: There's a little juice.

3. **Q:** _____
   A: There are 3 cups.

4. **Q:** _____
   A: There's a lot of fruit.

5. **Q:** _____
   A: There are 4 knives.

6. **Q:** _____
   A: There's a lot of bread.

3. Listening

Another group plans a picnic. How much or how many of each thing do they need? Write the number or check (✓) the correct column.

	Number	A few	A little	A lot
1. hot dogs	25	☐	☐	☐
2. fruit		☐	☐	☐
3. cheese		☐	☐	☐
4. pasta		☐	☐	☐
5. cups		☐	☐	☐
6. cookies		☐	☐	☐

Lessons 25 & 26 Mini-review

1. Language check

A Choose the correct words to complete the conversation.

Doctor Do you eat healthy food?
Michiko Well, yeah. I eat _a lot of_ (a lot of / a few) fruit.
Doctor How _____ (many / much) fruit do you eat in a week?
Michiko Well, I have a banana for breakfast every day, and I usually eat _____ (a few / a little) apples each week, too.
Doctor That's good. How _____ (many / much) soda do you drink?
Michiko I only drink _____ (a few / a little) soda. I know it's not good for me.
Doctor Great. How _____ (many / much) hot dogs do you eat in a week?
Michiko Oh, maybe about eight. I eat _____ (a lot of / a little) hot dogs.
Doctor Yes, you do! How about cookies?
Michiko Well, I don't like cookies, but I eat _____ (a few / a little) ice cream on Sundays.

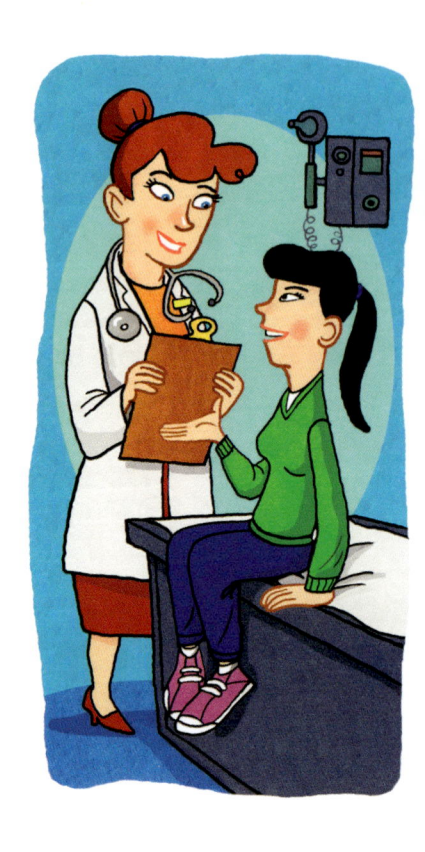

B Check (✓) four things you eat or drink. Put an ✗ next to four things you don't eat or drink. Then write sentences.

I eat eggs.
I don't eat meat.

1. _____
2. _____
3. _____
4. _____
5. _____
6. _____
7. _____
8. _____

☐ apples ☐ ice cream
☐ bananas ☐ juice
☐ bread ✗ meat
☐ broccoli ☐ milk
☐ butter ☐ pasta
✓ eggs ☐ potatoes
☐ hamburgers ☐ rice
☐ hot dogs ☐ water

90 Unit 7

C Answer these questions about yourself. Write a number or use *a lot*, *a little*, or *a few*.

1. How much rice do you eat in a week?
    I eat a lot of rice.
2. How many books do you have in your bag?
3. How much homework do you do every day?
4. How many T-shirts do you have?
5. How many magazines do you read in a month?
6. How much TV do you watch in a week?
7. How many DVDs do you have?
8. How much water do you drink every day?

2. Listening

Minnie and Amanda talk about what they need for a class party. Listen and check (✓) the correct answers.

1. There are _____ plates.
    - ☑ a lot of   ☐ a few
2. Minnie and Amanda have _____ students in their class.
    - ☐ 25   ☐ 20
3. There's _____ juice.
    - ☐ a few   ☐ a little
4. Minnie and Amanda need some _____ .
    - ☐ cookies   ☐ bananas and apples
5. _____ is Amanda's favorite food.
    - ☐ Fruit   ☐ Ice cream

Time for a Game?
See page 120.

What We Eat 91

Lesson 27: A snack

1. Vocabulary

A Look at the messy kitchen. Match the two parts of each sentence. Then listen and practice.

1. The chicken is ___e___
2. The jelly is _____
3. The ketchup is _____
4. The lettuce is _____
5. The mayonnaise is _____
6. The mustard is _____
7. The pepper is _____
8. The salt is _____

a. next to the salt.
b. next to the jelly.
c. behind the chicken.
d. in the cabinet.
e. in front of the ketchup.
f. next to the pepper.
g. next to the mustard.
h. on a plate.

B What do people put on the food items below? Write two things for each item. Use words from Part A or your own ideas.

1. sandwich: *mustard, lettuce*
2. eggs: _____
3. hamburger: _____
4. hot dog: _____
5. meat: _____

2. Language focus

A Wendy makes a sandwich. Listen and practice.

Wendy I'm hungry. Let's make a sandwich!
Luke Good idea. I'm hungry, too.
Wendy Um, there's some chicken here.
Luke Good! I like chicken sandwiches.
Wendy There's some mustard, but there isn't any mayonnaise.
Luke That's OK. Mustard is fine.
Wendy There's some pepper. Oh, no! There aren't any potatoes!
Luke What? Potatoes on a sandwich?
Wendy Sure! Oh, look! There are some bananas . . .
Luke What kind of sandwich is that?
Wendy It's my favorite! Do you want one?
Luke No, thanks. I'm not hungry now.

some / any
Countable nouns
There **are some** bananas.
There **aren't any** potatoes.
Uncountable nouns
There**'s some** mustard.
There **isn't any** mayonnaise.

B Look at the photos. Write sentences with *some* or *any*. Then listen and check.

1. *There isn't any salt.* (salt)
2. _____ (mustard)
3. _____ (eggs)
4. _____ (chicken)
5. _____ (apples)
6. _____ (cups)
7. _____ (bananas)
8. _____ (ketchup)

3. Speaking

Think of your refrigerator. Tell a classmate what is and what isn't in it. Use the words in the box or your own ideas.

> There's some juice. There isn't any water.

> There's some ice cream. There isn't any mustard.

juice milk ice cream
eggs ketchup mustard
meat apples chicken water

Lesson 28

On the menu

1. Vocabulary

A Look at the restaurant menu. Write the names of the items in the correct places on the menu. Then listen and practice.

T.121

Bob's DINER
Lunch Menu

Appetizers
- salad $3.00
- _____ $2.50
- _____ $2.50

Main Dishes
- hamburger $4.50
- _____ $5.00
- _____ $5.00
- chicken sandwich $6.00
- today's fish $4.50
- rice and beans with meat ... $6.50

☐ baked potato ☐ black bean soup ☐ cheeseburger

☐ steak sandwich ☐ vegetable soup

Side Orders
- French fries $2.00
- _____ $1.50

Desserts
- ice cream $1.50
- cookies $1.00
- _____ $2.00
- _____ $2.00
- _____ $2.00

Drinks
- soda $1.50
- _____ $2.00
- milk $1.00
- _____ $2.00

☐ carrot cake ☐ chocolate cake ☐ iced tea

☐ milk shake ☐ pie

B What are some of your favorite foods in a restaurant? Complete the chart. Then compare with your classmates.

Favorite appetizer	_____
Favorite main dish	_____
Favorite side order	_____
Favorite dessert	_____
Favorite drink	_____

What's your favorite appetizer?

My favorite appetizer is . . .

Unit 7

2. Language focus

A Tommy orders lunch. Listen and practice.

Server Hi. Are you ready to order?
Tommy Yes, I am.
Server OK. Would you like an appetizer?
Tommy Yes. I'd like vegetable soup, please.
Server OK. What else?
Tommy I'd like a chicken sandwich, please.
Server And would you like a side order?
Tommy No, thanks.
Server Would you like a drink?
Tommy Yes, please. I'd like a milk shake and some water. I'm really thirsty!

would like
I**'d like** vegetable soup, please.   **Would** you **like** a drink?   Yes, please. I**'d like** some water.   No, thanks.
I'd = I would

B Tommy orders dessert. Complete the conversation. Listen and check. Then practice.

Server _Would you like_ anything else?
Tommy Yes. _____ some cake.
Server What kind of cake _____ you _____?
Tommy _____ chocolate cake. And _____ some ice cream, too, please.
Server OK.
Tommy Oh! _____ some cookies, too.
Server Wow! That's a lot of dessert!

3. Pronunciation Intonation

Listen. Notice the intonation. Listen again and practice.

Would you like an appetizer?
Would you like a side order?
Would you like a drink?
Would you like anything else?

4. Listening

What do Ana, Kate, Rafael, and Zach order? Listen and write **A** (Ana), **K** (Kate), **R** (Rafael), or **Z** (Zach).

What We Eat

UNIT 7 Get Connected

Read

A Read the Web site quickly. Write the names of five foods in the text.

1. _____ 2. _____ 3. _____ 4. _____ 5. _____

---

www.cookingwithmarcelomontenegro.com

Cooking with Marcelo Montenegro

Marcelo Montenegro is from Minas Gerais, Brazil. He's only 17, and he's already a cooking **genius**. Marcello is very interested in cooking and he has more than 100 **cookbooks**! He has a cool blog – "Marcelo Montenegro Cooking" – where he **posts** his own recipes, photos, videos and cooking **tips**.

Marcelo doesn't just cook his own recipes, though. He also accepts **challenges** from his friends. So he takes his friends' favorite foods and creates new and sometimes very weird **recipes**. These include appetizers, main dishes, and desserts. Would you like a stroganoff pizza recipe? Or maybe a salad with strawberries and cheese? Pasta hamburger with ketchup and pepper? These are just some examples of the creative combinations you can find on his blog. There are also some special recipes with chocolate – one of Marcelo's favorite foods. And Marcelo gives some great **nutrition** tips. Check out his blog the next time you cook.

More Vocabulary Practice? See page 125.

B 🎧 T.126 Read the Web site slowly. Check your answers in Part A.

C Are these statements true or false? Write *True* or *False*. Then correct the false statements.

1. Marcelo Montenegro doesn't like cookbooks.
   False.   _He has more than 100 cookbooks._

2. Marcelo has a TV show.
   _____

3. He only cooks his own recipes.
   _____

4. Marcelo's favorite food is pizza.
   _____

5. There are cooking and nutrition tips on his blog.
   _____

96 Unit 7

It's only pasta!

Listen

A 🎧 T.127 Nick and Rachel talk about cooking. Listen and answer the questions.

1. What do Nick and Rachel want to make?
   They want to make some pasta.
2. How many tomatoes do they have? _____
3. How much cheese is there? _____
4. How much pasta is there? _____
5. How many cans of soup are there? _____

B What do you think? Answer the questions. Give reasons.

1. Do you think cooking with friends is fun? _____
2. Do you think cooking is easy or difficult? _____
3. Do you think it's a good idea to use a cookbook? _____
4. Would you like to be a good cook? _____

Your turn

Write

A Think about a dish you like to make. Complete the chart.

Name of the dish	
Things you need to make it	
How much you need	

B Write about making a dish. Use the answers in Part A to help you.

I can make _____ . *It's really delicious! You need*

_____

_____

_____

What We Eat 97

UNIT 7 Review

Language chart review

Countable and uncountable nouns	
Countable	**Uncountable**
Specific: There are **two apples**. General: I love **apples**.	There's **broccoli** on the table. I don't like **broccoli**.

How much / How many . . . ?	
With countable	**With uncountable**
How many apples do we need? We need **a few** apples. We need **three** apples.	**How much** bread do we have? We have **a little** bread. We have **a lot of** bread.

some / any
Countable nouns
There **are some** cups. There **aren't any** plates.
Uncountable nouns
There's **some** salt. There **isn't any** rice.

A Betty and Jacob make breakfast for their family. Complete the conversation.

Betty Let's make breakfast.

Jacob Good idea. How about eggs? We all like ___eggs___ (eggs / ten eggs).

Betty OK. _____ (How much / How many) eggs do we need?

Jacob Well, I think we need eight eggs. And we need _____ (a little / a few) cheese, too.

Betty We don't have _____ (some / any) cheese.

Jacob Oh. So let's put _____ (a little / a few) potatoes in the eggs.

Betty But Mom doesn't like _____ (potatoes / the potatoes) in her eggs.

Jacob That's true. How about _____ (a little / a lot) chicken? There's _____ (some / any) chicken in the refrigerator.

Betty Yes! And let's put _____ (some / any) milk in the eggs, too. _____ (How much / How many) milk do we need?

Jacob We just need _____ (a little / a few) milk. Do we want bread, too?

Betty Yes, we do. And there's _____ (a lot / a lot of) bread here.

Jacob OK! Let's cook!

B Write questions about Betty and Jacob with *How much* or *How many*. Then look again at the picture in Part A, and answer the questions. Use *a few, a little,* or *a lot of*.

1. milk
   Q: How much milk do they have?
   A: They have a little milk.

2. potatoes
   Q: _____
   A: _____

3. chicken
   Q: _____
   A: _____

4. fruit
   Q: _____
   A: _____

5. bread
   Q: _____
   A: _____

6. eggs
   Q: _____
   A: _____

Language chart review

would like

I'd like a sandwich.
Would you **like** a side order?
   Yes, please. **I'd like** french fries.
   No, thanks.

C Molly orders lunch. Complete the questions. Then write answers. Use the sentences in the box.

☐ I'd like a chicken sandwich.
☐ I'd like chocolate ice cream.
☐ No, thanks.
☑ Yes. I'd like a sandwich.
☐ Yes. I'd like some ice cream.
☐ Yes, please. I'd like apple juice.

Server Hi. Are you ready to order?
Molly Yes. I'd like a sandwich.
Server What kind of sandwich ___would___ you ___like___ ?
Molly _____
Server _____ a side dish? Maybe some french fries?
Molly _____
Server Would you like a drink?
Molly _____
Server _____ you _____ dessert?
Molly _____
Server What kind of ice cream _____ ?
Molly _____

Time for the Theme Project?
See page 132.

What We Eat 99

Lesson 29: World weather

1. Vocabulary

A Match the symbols to the sentences describing weather and temperature. Then listen and practice.

Weather

1. ☀ _d_ a. It's cloudy.
2. 🌬 ___ b. It's rainy.
3. ❄ ___ c. It's snowy.
4. ☁ ___ d. It's sunny.
5. 🌧 ___ e. It's windy.

Temperature

6. 🌡 ___ f. It's cold.
7. 🌡 ___ g. It's cool.
8. 🌡 ___ h. It's hot.
9. 🌡 ___ i. It's warm.

B It's December. Look at the weather map, and complete the sentences with words from Part A. Then listen and practice.

1. It's _cold_ and _snowy_ in Moscow.
2. It's _____ and _____ in Chicago.
3. It's _____ and _____ in Tokyo.
4. It's _____ and _____ in Rio de Janeiro.
5. It's _____ and _____ in Cape Town.

C What kind of weather do you like?
What kind of weather don't you like?
Tell your classmates.

> I like hot, sunny weather. I don't like . . .

UNIT 8 The Natural World

2. Language focus

A It's Sunday afternoon. Tommy is in an online chat room. Listen and practice.

> **What's the weather like?**
> **What's the weather like** in April?
> It's usually **rainy**.
> **What's the weather like** today?
> It's **warm** and **sunny** today.

International Chat

Tommy: Hi, everyone! I'm doing my science homework. I need information about April weather around the world.
Josie: Hi, Tommy! I can help you.
Tommy: Great! Where do you live, Josie?
Josie: In Santiago, Chile.
Tommy: What's the weather like in Santiago in April?
Josie: It's usually warm. But it's not warm today.
Tommy: What's the weather like today?
Josie: It's hot and sunny. I want to go to the park later.
Tommy: That sounds fun! Thanks for your help! Sofia, can you help me, too? Where do you live?

Now in chat room:
- Tommy
- Sofia
- Lynn
- Garth
- Josie

B Complete more of Tommy's questions and answers from the chat. Listen and check. Then practice.

1. **Tommy** What's the weather like in Chicago in April?
   Sofia *It's usually warm and rainy.*
2. **Tommy** What's the weather like in New York in April?
   Lynn _____ and _____ .
3. **Tommy** What's the weather _____ in New York today?
   Lynn _____ and _____ today.
4. **Tommy** _____ in Winnipeg in April?
   Garth _____ and _____ .
5. **Garth** _____ in Darwin in April?
   Tommy _____ and _____ , but it's cool and cloudy now.

3. Speaking

Work with a classmate. Ask and answer questions about the weather in your town or city in different months.

> What's the weather like in Rio in February?

> It's usually hot and sunny.

Lesson 30 — Natural wonders

1. Vocabulary

A Complete the sentences with the words in the box. Then listen and practice.

- ☐ the Andes Mountains
- ☐ the Galápagos Islands
- ☑ Mammoth Hot Springs
- ☐ El Yunque Rain Forest
- ☐ the Jenolan Caves
- ☐ the Mississippi River

1. _Mammoth Hot Springs_ are in Yellowstone National Park in the United States.
2. Some people live on houseboats on _____ . 
3. _____ are in the Pacific Ocean. 
4. _____ are in Australia. 
5. _____ is in Puerto Rico. 
6. People ski in _____ . 

B Kate loves the outdoors. Complete her sentences with the words in the box.

- ☐ cave
- ☐ hot spring
- ☐ island
- ☐ mountain
- ☐ rain forest
- ☑ river

1. I want to go canoeing on a ___river___ .
2. I want to climb a really big _____ .
3. I want to take a boat ride around an _____ in the sea.
4. I want to take pictures of birds and other animals in a _____ .
5. I want to see the inside of a big, underground _____ .
6. I want to sit and relax in a _____ .

102 Unit 8

2. Language focus

A Kate visits Yellowstone National Park. She's talking with a guide. Listen and practice.

Guide You can see a lot of amazing things in this park.
Kate So, what can you see on this trail?
Guide You can see some incredible mountains, hot springs, rivers . . .
Kate Can you see any animals?
Guide Yes, you can. You can see snakes and wolves. And sometimes you can see bears.
Kate I don't want to see any bears right now!
Guide And they don't want to see you!
Kate I'm hungry. Can you buy any food around here?
Guide No, you can't. You can buy food at hotels and at the souvenir shops. You were supposed to bring lunch!
Kate Oh, no! I forgot!

can (for possibility)

You **can** see a lot of amazing things.
What **can you** see on this trail?
  You **can** see some incredible mountains.
Can you buy any food around here?
  Yes, **you can**.
  No, **you can't**.

B What can you do at these parks? Look at the chart, and write sentences. Then listen and check.

Park Facilities and Activities	🚣	🎣	⛺	🐦	🏊
Kent Park	✓		✓	✓	
Ranch Park		✓	✓		
Thunder Park	✓			✓	✓

1. (Kent Park) <u>You can go canoeing. You can go camping. You can see birds.</u>
2. (Ranch Park) _____
3. (Thunder Park) _____

3. Listening

Can people do these activities near Kate's hometown? Listen and check (✓) Yes or No.

	Yes	No
1. go canoeing	✓	☐
2. climb mountains	☐	☐
3. visit caves	☐	☐
4. go to hot springs	☐	☐
5. go dancing	☐	☐

The Natural World 103

Lessons 29 & 30 Mini-review

1. Language check

A Look at the weather map for the United States and Canada. Write questions and answers about the weather in the cities.

Today's Weather

1. (Montreal) _What's the weather like in Montreal?_
   It's cold and snowy.
2. (Orlando) _____
   _____
3. (New York) _____
   _____
4. (Seattle) _____
   _____
5. (Phoenix) _____
   _____

B Match the words to complete the sentences.

1. You can sit and relax in that __c__ .   a. caves
2. You can go canoeing on that _____ .   b. beach
3. You can climb that _____ .   c. hot spring
4. You can go underground in those _____ .   d. mountain
5. You can go dancing in _____ .   e. river
6. You can go swimming at the _____ .   f. town

104   Unit 8

C Jesse and his father talk about vacation plans. Complete their conversation with *you can*, *you can't*, *what can you*, and *can you*.

Jesse I don't know, Dad. The park sounds a little boring.
Mr. Willis Boring? The park sounds really interesting!
Jesse But *what can you* do there?
Mr. Willis _____ do a lot of things. _____ hike and camp . . .
Jesse You can hike and camp here in our town!
Mr. Willis Yes, _____. But _____ climb mountains in our town? _____ see caves in our town?
Jesse No, _____. Maybe the park is OK. _____ see bats in the caves?
Mr. Willis Yes, and _____ see them fly out of the caves at night. There's also a great beach.
Jesse _____ do at the beach?
Mr. Willis _____ go swimming. Or _____ take a boat ride to an island.
Jesse OK. I want to go. Let's tell Mom we have a plan!

2. Listening

Jesse and his father watch *Adventure Vacations* on TV. This week's show is in northern Japan. Listen and number the places in the correct order.

____ cave
____ hot spring
____ island
_1_ mountain
____ river

Time for a Game?
See page 121.

The Natural World 105

Lesson 31

World of friends

1. Vocabulary

A Can you say "hello" in other languages? Match the languages to the correct greetings. Then listen and practice.

1. Arabic _c_
2. German ____
3. Greek ____
4. Italian ____
5. Portuguese ____
6. Russian ____

a. Buon giorno!
b. Olá!
c. Ahalan!
d. Geia sou!
e. Zdravstvuite!
f. Guten Tag!

B Tommy meets a lot of friends online. Where are they from? Complete their sentences with the words in the box. Then listen and practice.

☐ Germany ☐ Greece ☐ Italy ☑ Morocco ☐ Portugal ☐ Russia

1. My name is Khalil. I live in _Morocco_. "Ahalan!"

2. I'm Karl. I live in _____. "Guten Tag!"

3. "Buon giorno!" I'm Carlotta. I live in _____.

4. "Geia sou!" I'm Christina. I live in _____.

5. I'm Ivan. I live in _____. "Zdravstvuite!"

6. I'm Emilia. I live in _____. "Olá!"

C Work with a classmate. Look at Part B. Ask and answer questions about where Tommy's friends are from and what languages they speak.

- Is Ivan from Russia?
- Yes, he is.

- Does Emilia speak Italian?
- No, she doesn't. She speaks Portuguese.

106 Unit 8

2. Language focus

A Claudia wants new e-pals. She asks Tommy about his online friends. Listen and practice.

Claudia Can you help me find some new e-pals?
Tommy Well, maybe you can write to my e-pals. Karl, Emilia, Ivan, and Carlotta are really interesting.
Claudia Do they like sports?
Tommy Sure. One of them plays tennis, two of them play soccer, and . . .
Claudia Who plays soccer?
Tommy Karl and Emilia do. Karl lives in Germany. The others live in Greece, Morocco, Italy . . .
Claudia Oh! Who lives in Italy?
Tommy Carlotta does.
Claudia Great! I'll write to Karl and Carlotta. I love soccer, and I want to learn German and Italian.

> **Who + (verb) . . . ?**
> Who **lives** in Italy?
> Carlotta **does**.
> Who **plays** soccer?
> Karl and Emilia **do**.

B Read these messages from Tommy's newest e-pals. Write questions and answers. Listen and check. Then practice.

From: Khalil
I like music, and I watch a lot of American movies. I go camping a lot. Do you like to go camping?

From: Christina
I live near beautiful islands. You can swim and relax on the beach. I like music. I play the guitar and the piano.

1. Who lives near beautiful islands?   *Christina does.*
2. Who watches movies?   _____
3. Who plays the guitar?   _____
4. _____   Khalil does.
5. _____   Both Christina and Khalil do.

3. Listening

Tommy talks about his e-pals, Ivan, Emilia, and Christina. Who does these things? Listen and check (✓) the correct name or names.

	Ivan	Emilia	Christina
1. take photographs	☐	☐	☐
2. speak four languages	☐	☐	☐
3. swim every day	☐	☐	☐
4. play the guitar	☐	☐	☐

Lesson 32: International Day

1. Vocabulary

A Listen and practice.

100 one hundred	167 one hundred and sixty-seven
1,000 one thousand	2,412 two thousand, four hundred and twelve
10,000 ten thousand	85,000 eighty-five thousand
100,000 one hundred thousand	960,102 nine hundred sixty thousand, one hundred and two

B Listen and practice.

☐ 154   ☐ 17,000   ☐ 20,000   ☑ 25,000   ☐ 90,000   ☐ 100,000

C This Sunday is International Day at school. Students are giving presentations. Listen and complete their sentences with the correct numbers from the box in Part B.

1. Every year, _25,000_ people run from Sydney to Bondi Beach in the Fun Run. (Australia)

2. There are _____ kinds of birds in my country. (Colombia)

3. There are _____ people in the city of Guaynabo. (Puerto Rico)

4. _____ people can watch a soccer game in Maracanã Stadium. (Brazil)

5. There are _____ national forests in the United States. (U.S.A.)

6. There are _____ "Mounties" – a special group of police officers – in Canada. (Canada)

2. Language focus

What + (noun) . . . ?

What subjects do you like?
I like math and science.
What sports does he like?
He doesn't like sports.
What sports do they play?
They play all sports.

A Zach's father, Mr. Baker, asks Claudia some questions. Listen and practice.

T.145

Mr. Baker Great presentation, Claudia! Are there really 17,000 species of birds in the Colombian rain forest?
Claudia At least! Some scientists think there are 20,000. And there are 130,000 species of plants.
Mr. Baker You know a lot, Claudia! What school subjects do you like?
Claudia I like math and science.
Mr. Baker And Zach says you're athletic. What sports do you play?
Claudia Well, I play soccer, Ping-Pong, basketball, tennis . . .
Mr. Baker Wow! And your brother? What sports does he like?
Claudia He doesn't like sports.
Mr. Baker What about your parents? What sports do they play?
Claudia Well, they play tennis and golf. My father plays golf 365 days a year!

B Now Mr. Baker talks with Rafael. Complete their conversation. Listen and check. Then practice.

T.146

Mr. Baker _What sports_ do you like, Rafael?
Rafael I like soccer, tennis, and basketball. How about you? _____, Mr. Baker?
Mr. Baker Oh, I like all sports, especially baseball.
Rafael I want to introduce you to my father, but his English isn't very good.
Mr. Baker _____ speak? Portuguese?
Rafael Yes. _____ Portuguese and some Spanish.
Mr. Baker Great! I speak a little Spanish, too. Let's find him!

3. Speaking

Ask your classmates questions. Use the words in the box or your own ideas.

colors   music groups   subjects   video games
foods   sports   TV shows

What sports do you like?   I like basketball.

The Natural World 109

UNIT 8 Get Connected

Read

A Read the article quickly. Check (✓) the main idea.

☐ 1. The air is dirty and the oceans are rising.

☐ 2. Global warming is a big problem, but everyone can help.

☐ 3. It's hotter these days and many animals are dying.

Global Warming

Look around you. What's the weather like these days? In many places like Antarctica and Greenland it's usually cold, but now it's hotter. The ice in these cold places is **melting**, and the water in the oceans is **rising**. The air is **dirty**. Many species of plants and animals are **dying**. This is a serious problem and it has a name – *global warming*.

Can we stop global warming? Yes, we can. Scientists think there's still time to **save** our incredible planet. So, what can we do? Here are some ideas:

- Use less water, paper, and electricity.
- Walk, bike, or take the bus – don't drive.
- **Recycle** paper and **plastic** items.
- Ask your classmates, friends, and family for ideas.

And don't forget . . . our actions can save the world for many years to come. Let's start today.

More Vocabulary Practice? See page 125.

B 🎧 T.147 Read the article slowly. Check your answer in Part A.

C Answer the questions.

1. What's the weather usually like in Greenland? *It's usually cold.*
2. What's the ice doing in cold places? _____
3. What's the air like around the world? _____
4. Can we stop global warming? _____
5. What can you do to help? Name one thing. _____

That's a really serious problem.

A Jeff and Isabel talk about their projects. Listen and answer the questions.

1. What's Isabel making? _She's making a poster._
2. Who's doing a project for the science fair? _____
3. Who can enter the recycling contest? _____
4. What can the winners of the contest do? _____
5. Who wants to enter the contest? _____

B What do you think? Answer the questions. Give reasons.

1. Do you think global warming is a serious problem? _____
2. Is recycling a good idea? _____
3. Do you think students can help save the planet? _____
4. Would you like to enter a recycling contest? _____
5. Do you think TV shows about our planet are interesting? _____

Your turn

A Think about some things you can do to help our planet. Answer the questions.

1. What do you think about global warming? _____
2. What's one thing you can do to help? _____
3. What's one thing your family can do to help? _____
4. What can you and your classmates do to help? _____
5. Do you think there's still time to save our planet? _____

B Write about your plans to help the planet. Use the answers in Part A to help you.

I think global warming is _____

The Natural World

UNIT 8 Review

Language chart review

Who + (verb) . . . ?
Who goes camping a lot?
I **do**.
Pablo **does**.
Sarah and Tim **do**.

What + (noun) . . . ?
What colors do you like?
I like blue and yellow.
What languages does he speak?
He speaks French and Italian.

A Look at the pictures. Write questions and answers about the people.

Ken

Vicky

Sonya and Miguel

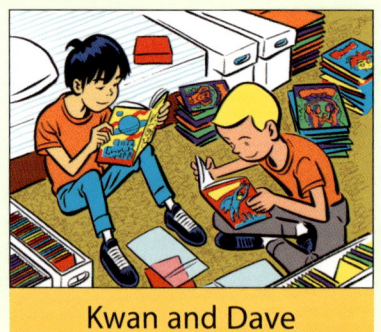

Marc

Kwan and Dave

Betsy

1. speak Italian
   Q: *Who speaks Italian?*   **A:** *Ken does.*
2. have a pet parrot
   Q: _____   **A:** _____
3. eat a lot of ice cream
   Q: _____   **A:** _____
4. live on a houseboat
   Q: _____   **A:** _____
5. like to play soccer
   Q: _____   **A:** _____
6. collect comic books
   Q: _____   **A:** _____

B Look again at Part A. Write **What** questions with the words. Then answer the questions.

1. dessert / Betsy / like
   Q: *What dessert does Betsy like?* A: *She likes ice cream.*
2. instrument / Marc / play
   Q: _____ A: _____
3. game / Sonya and Miguel / like
   Q: _____ A: _____
4. languages / Ken / speak
   Q: _____ A: _____
5. sport / Vicky / play
   Q: _____ A: _____
6. color / Kwan and Dave / like
   Q: _____ A: _____

Language chart review

What's the weather like?	can (for possibility)
What's the weather like? It's usually **sunny**. **What's the weather like?** It's **cool** and **rainy**.	What **can you** do here? **You can** go hiking. **Can you** see any animals? Yes, **you can**. / No, **you can't**.

C Betsy asks Sonya about life on a houseboat. Look again at the language charts. Then complete the conversation.

Betsy Do you like living on a houseboat in Florida, Sonya?
Sonya Well, yes, I do. It's a lot of fun.
Betsy What's it like? What *can you* do on a houseboat?
Sonya A lot of things! _____ go swimming, and _____ go canoeing.
Betsy _____ the weather _____ in Florida? Is it always warm?
Sonya Yes, it's usually warm. Actually, today it's very hot!
Betsy Wow! What _____ do in Florida?
Sonya Well, _____ visit Miami. It's a great city.
Betsy What _____ do there?
Sonya _____ go to the Miami Aquarium. It's an interesting place.
Betsy What _____ see there?
Sonya _____ see a lot of fish and learn about the ocean.
Betsy Wow! That's fascinating. I want to go to Florida.

Time for the Theme Project?
See page 133.

UNIT 1 Game *What's wrong?*

Work with a classmate. What's wrong with the picture? Write sentences with the words in the box. The pair that finishes first is the winner.

☐ bed	☐ guitar	☑ sandwich	☐ sneakers
☐ bicycle	☐ pizza	☐ skirt	☐ soccer balls

1. *There's a sandwich in the home store.*
2. _____
3. _____
4. _____
5. _____
6. _____
7. _____
8. _____

UNIT 2 Game *Who is it?*

Read what these students do in their free time. Then play a game with a classmate.

Classmate 1 Choose a person in the picture. Don't tell your classmate. Answer Classmate 2's questions.

Classmate 2 Classmate 1 is thinking of a person in the picture. Ask Classmate 1 questions. Guess the person.

Classmate 2 Do you watch DVDs?
Classmate 1 Yes, I do.
Classmate 2 Are you Miyoko?
Classmate 1 No, I'm not.
Classmate 2 Do you take guitar lessons?
Classmate 1 Yes, I do.
Classmate 2 Are you Eric?
Classmate 1 Yes, I am.

Miyoko
I take guitar lessons.
I listen to music.
I in-line skate.
I play video games.
I draw pictures.

Felix
I watch DVDs.
I hang out at the mall.
I talk on the phone.
I read books.
I draw pictures.

Bruno
I collect trading cards.
I listen to music.
I use the Internet.
I play video games.
I read magazines.

Eric
I watch DVDs.
I take guitar lessons.
I use the Internet.
I play soccer.
I hang out with my friends.

Janice
I collect trading cards.
I talk on the phone.
I play video games.
I read books.
I hang out with my friends.

Lucia
I hang out at the mall.
I take guitar lessons.
I in-line skate.
I play soccer.
I read magazines.

UNIT 3 Game *Play ball!*

A Work with a classmate. Read the clues. Then write the correct words on the ball. The pair that finishes first is the winner.

a. A biker wears a _____ on his or her head.

b. A lot of people do _____ in Asia.

c. Skateboarders wear knee _____ .

d. Tennis players wear _____ on their feet.

e. People _____ at the beach.

f. You can _____ in a park.

g. A baseball player has a _____ .

h. Each player wears a _____ with a number.

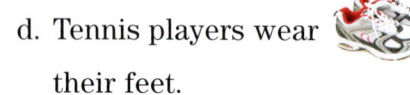

i.  _____ is a fun sport.

j.  _____ teams play on a field.

k. People _____ in a pool or at the beach.

l. People wear gloves on their _____ .

B Write each numbered letter from the puzzle. Then write the answer.

Q: __ _h_ __ __ __ __ __ __ __ __ __
    1 2 3 4 5 6 7 8 9 10

__ __ __ __ __ __ _t_ __ __ __ __ __ __ ?
11 12 13 14 15 16 17 18 19 20 21 22 23

A: _____

UNIT 4 Game *All about music*

Play the game with a classmate. Use things in your bag as game markers. Use a coin to find out how many spaces to move. Heads = 1, Tails = 2.

- Take turns. Flip a coin and move your marker to the correct space.
- Complete the sentence or follow the directions.
- The person who gets to FINISH first, wins.

START

I think country music is _____.

A music CD costs _____.

You win a music contest! **Take another turn.**

The name of a hip-hop singer is _____.

Ask a classmate a question.

A rock band I like is _____.

My favorite singer or group is _____.

Ask a classmate a question.

Five kinds of music are _____.

My classmate's favorite singer or group is _____. (Ask him or her.)

_____ is my favorite kind of music. I like it a lot.

You are very musical. **Take another turn.**

You are late for music class. **Lose a turn.**

I think _____ music is boring. I don't like it at all.

A famous singer, musician, or group from my country is _____.

Tell a classmate two groups you like.

My mother's or father's favorite kind of music is _____.

A rock group I don't like is _____.

FINISH

UNIT 5   Game *What are they doing?*

A Look at the picture for one minute. Then cover the picture, and read the sentences. Check (✓) T (true) or F (false).

	T	F
1. Paul is buying a baseball glove.	☐	✓
2. Sarah is watching TV.	☐	☐
3. Kevin is wearing a helmet.	☐	☐
4. Ann is doing karate.	☐	☐
5. Will is throwing trash in the trash can.	☐	☐
6. Ms. Kean and Mr. Cardoso are taking pictures.	☐	☐
7. Dmitri is talking on the phone.	☐	☐
8. Adam and Suzanne are swimming.	☐	☐
9. Adela is playing the violin.	☐	☐

B Work with a classmate. Close your book. Your classmate's book is open. How many things can you remember from the picture? Tell your classmate. Your classmate says *Yes* or *No*. Then switch roles.

— John is reading a book.
— No, he isn't. He's listening to music.

118   Unit 5 Game

UNIT 6   Game *X and O*

A Play the game with a classmate. Take turns.

One person is *X* and one person is *O*. *X* starts.
Classmate X Point to a picture. Ask *Where's / Where are* _____ *going?*
Classmate O Answer the question.
▶ Is the answer correct? Mark the picture with an *O*.
▶ Not correct? Do not mark the picture.

Now Classmate O points to a picture and asks a question. Classmate X answers. Continue playing until all the pictures are marked *X* or *O*. The player with the most marks wins.

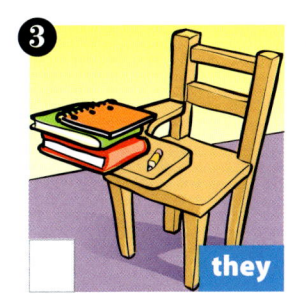

1. he
2. she
3. they
4. she
5. he
6. you
7. he
8. they
9. you
10. he
11. she
12. you

B These people are all on a bus. Where are they going? Complete the sentences.

1. Bill *is going to the circus* _____.
2. Jed and Mindy _____.
3. Henry _____.
4. Carl _____.
5. Pierre and Paulette _____.

Unit 6 Game   119

UNIT 7 Game *Food puzzle*

Work with a partner. Look at the photos. Guess the names of the items, and label the photos. Then write the names of the food items to complete the puzzle. The pair that finishes first is the winner.

ACROSS

2.
5.
6.
7.

DOWN

1. fruit
2.
3.
4.
5.
8.

120 Unit 7 Game

UNIT 8   Game *What's the weather like?*

Play the game with a classmate. Use things in your bag as game markers.
Use a coin to find out how many spaces to move. Heads = 1, Tails = 2.

- Take turns. Flip a coin and move your marker to the correct space.

Classmate 1 Ask a question about the weather, using the words in the space.

Classmate 2 Answer the question.

June. What's the weather like in June?   It's usually warm and rainy.

- The person who gets to FINISH first, wins.

START	June	September	Today	May
January	Today	February	October	March
April	December	June	August	Today
FINISH	November	October	September	July

Unit 8 Game   121

Get Connected Vocabulary Practice

UNIT 1

Complete the sentences with the words in the box.

☐ apartment building	☐ boy band	☑ lead singer	☐ music videos	☐ special	☐ typical

1. My friend is the main singer in the band. He's the ____lead singer____ .
2. His cousin plays in the band, too. He lives in a big _____ with more than 164 apartments.
3. Many people in his building have dogs and cats. They're _____ pets.
4. Look at this new album. There are no girls in this band. It's a _____ .
5. They like their English teacher a lot. She's a very kind and _____ person to them.
6. Brian likes to watch _____ on the Internet. The musicians sing, dance, and act.

UNIT 2

The underlined words belong in other sentences. Write the words where they belong.

1. That company has a lot of good review (v.) ideas. ____marketing____
2. There's a quiz tomorrow. Can you help me marketing (n.)? _____
3. That's a great creator (n.). They make very good computer games. _____
4. Do you answer all of your e-mail company (n.) every day? _____
5. This computer check out (v.) helps me study math. _____
6. That man is the messages (n.) of a really cool video game. _____
7. Software (n.) this cool video game. Look! You can play it online. _____

122 Get Connected Vocabulary Practice

UNIT 3

Complete the sentences with the words in the box.

1. She's the new <u>world champion</u> skateboarder.
2. Her positive attitude is a good example for other students.
   She's a _____ .
3. Suzie is an _____ , but she has many cousins.
4. They play together on the same team. They're _____ .
5. You can win _____ at our school's Sports Day.

- ☐ medals (n.)
- ☐ only child (n.)
- ☐ role model (n.)
- ☐ teammates (n.)
- ☑ world champion (adj.)

UNIT 4

Complete the advertisement with the words in the box.

- ☐ album (n.)
- ☐ download (v.)
- ☑ have (v.)
- ☐ sell (v.)
- ☐ convenient (adj.)
- ☐ e-books (n.)
- ☐ million (n.)
- ☐ visit (v.)

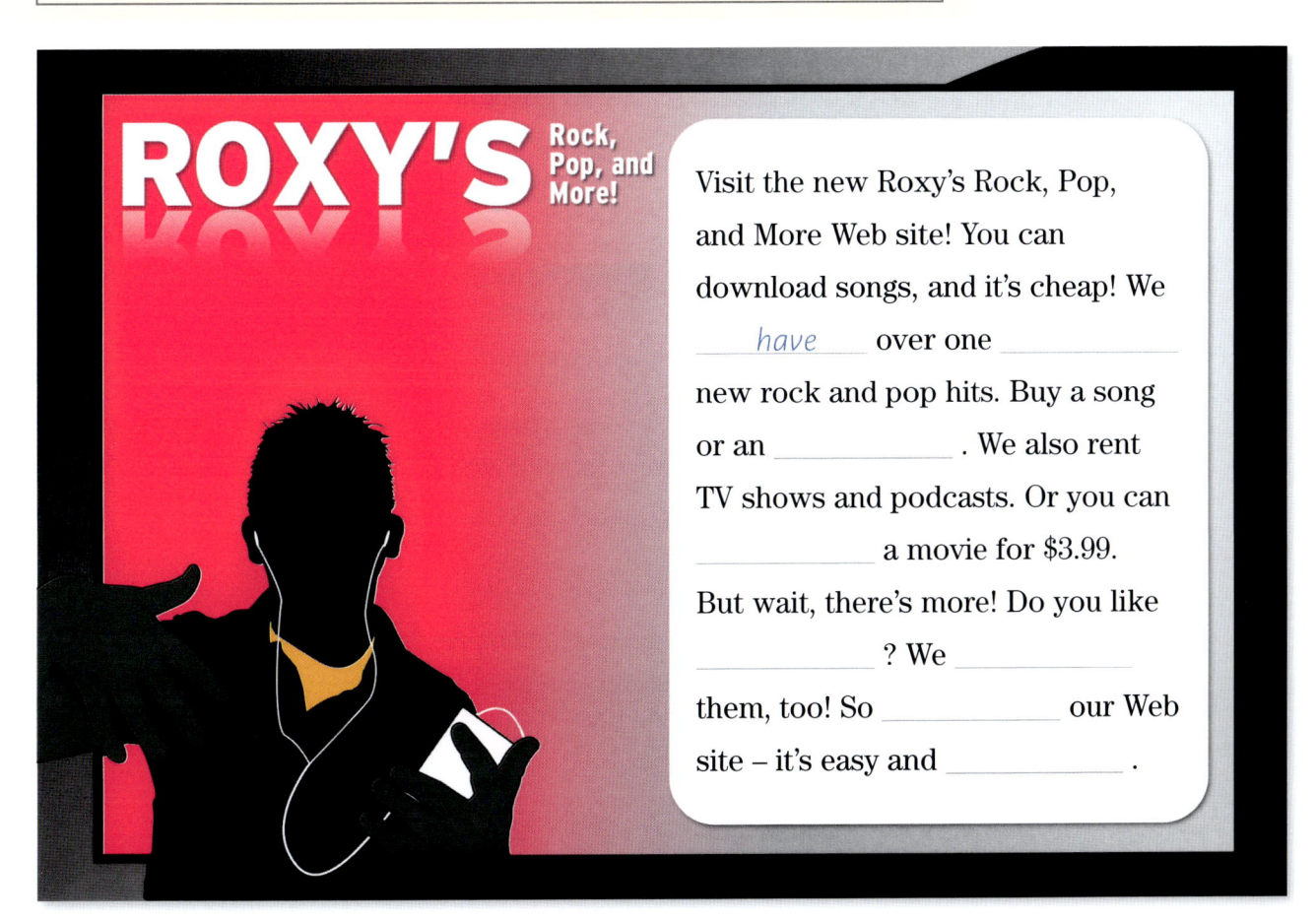

ROXY'S Rock, Pop, and More!

Visit the new Roxy's Rock, Pop, and More Web site! You can download songs, and it's cheap! We <u>have</u> over one _____ new rock and pop hits. Buy a song or an _____ . We also rent TV shows and podcasts. Or you can _____ a movie for $3.99. But wait, there's more! Do you like _____ ? We _____ them, too! So _____ our Web site – it's easy and _____ .

Get Connected Vocabulary Practice 123

UNIT 5

Circle the correct words to complete the sentences.

1. My little sister has a lot of very cute ((dolls)/ peaches).
2. We have tickets to walk around in that old (play / castle). It's very big.
3. I love this candy. It's (traditional / delicious)!
4. Buy two (tickets / dolls) at the movie theater.
5. Let's dance to this (delicious / traditional) Mexican song.
6. The actors in that (castle / play) are very good.
7. Apples, bananas, and (candy / peaches) are healthy foods.

UNIT 6

Complete the sentences with the words in the box.

☐ butter (n.) ☐ cows (n.) ☐ farm (n.) ☐ pounds (n.) ☐ weighs (v.) ☑ wire (n.)

1. That _____wire_____ is for Ken's new radio-controlled airplane.
2. I want to buy two _____ of potatoes to make some potato salad.
3. _____ give us milk.
4. Do you like _____ on your popcorn?
5. My mother isn't heavy. She only _____ 120 pounds.
6. My aunt and uncle live on a _____. They have lots of animals.

124 Get Connected Vocabulary Practice

UNIT 7

Complete the sentences with the words in the box.

- ☑ cookbook (n.)
- ☐ post (v.)
- ☐ sections (n.)
- ☐ nutrition (n.)
- ☐ recipe (n.)
- ☐ tips (n.)

1. He's a famous cook. His new __cookbook__ has a lot of great dishes in it.
2. Many people like to _____ new pictures on the Internet every day.
3. She writes for a Web site every week. She writes _____ about teen fashion.
4. It's a very big cookbook! There are ten _____ in it.
5. There's a lot of sugar in candy and soda. They aren't very healthy. There isn't much _____ in them.
6. That cookbook has an amazing _____ for chocolate cake. I want to make it.

UNIT 8

What sentence is next? Match the sentences on the left with the sentences on the right.

1. Clean up your room. _f_
2. You have a lot of paper. ____
3. It's hot today. Hurry up and eat your ice cream. ____
4. There's more water in the oceans these days. ____
5. The neighbor's pet snake is very sick. ____
6. The soda is in the refrigerator. ____
7. Give those plants water! ____

a. It's in that **plastic** (adj.) bottle.
b. They're **dying** (v.)!
c. The water is **rising** (v.).
d. Can someone **save** (v.) it?
e. It's **melting** (v.).
f. It's really **dirty** (adj.).
g. **Recycle** (v.) it!

UNIT 1

Theme Project: Make a poster about things you like and things you're good at.
Theme: Citizenship
Goal: To create stronger relationships in your classroom community

At Home

Read about Valeria.

> Hi! I'm Valeria Dias, and I'm 14. I'm athletic. I'm pretty good at soccer and volleyball. I'm also good at dancing. I like sports very much. I like gym a lot, too.

Complete the chart. Use your dictionary, if necessary.

Things I'm good at	Things I like
1.	1.
2.	2.
3.	3.

Draw pictures or bring photos of the things you are good at and the things you like to class.

In Class

- Make a poster. Use the sample poster as a model.

- Tell your group about the things you are good at and the things you like.

  > I'm musical. I'm good at the piano and the violin. I'm pretty good at English, too. I like . . .

- Display the posters in your classroom. Walk around and look at all of them. Who likes the same things you like? Who's good at the same things you're good at?

Things I'm good at | **Things I like**

I'm musical. I'm good at the piano and the violin. I'm pretty good at English, too. I like cats. I like math a lot. I like basketball, too.

_____
(name)

Sample poster

126   Unit 1 Theme Project

UNIT 2

Theme Project: Make a booklet about teachers in your school.
Theme: Citizenship
Goal: To become better acquainted with your school community

At Home

Read about Mr. Ramos.

This is Mr. Ramos. He teaches science. He gets up at 6:30 a.m. He eats breakfast at home. Then he goes to school. He doesn't go home at 2:30 p.m. – he coaches soccer after school. He eats dinner with his family at 6:30 p.m. He plays with his son in the evening. He reads in his free time.

Mr. Ramos

Before Class

Talk to a teacher at your school. Ask questions and complete the chart. Use your dictionary, if necessary.

	Name	Subject	Morning	Afternoon	Evening	Free time
Questions:			Do you eat breakfast at school?			
Answers:						

Draw a picture or bring a photo of the teacher to class.

In Class

Look at all the charts. Choose two teachers.

Make a page for each teacher. Use the sample page as a model.

Choose a group leader. Present your teachers to another group.

> This is Mrs. White. She teaches art class. She eats . . .

Give your group's pages to the teacher. The teacher staples together the pages.

Pass around the booklet. Which teacher do you want to know more about?

This is Mrs. White. She teaches art class. She eats breakfast at home. She goes to school at 7:30 a.m. She goes home at 4:00 p.m. She eats dinner at 7:00 p.m. Then she helps her children with their homework. She goes to the movies in her free time.

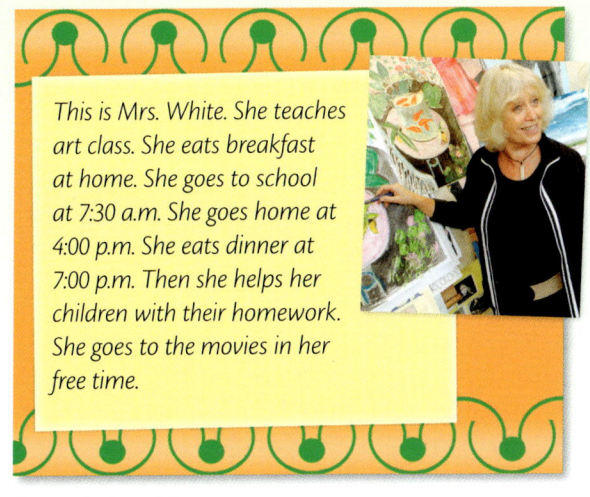

Sample booklet page

UNIT 3

Theme Project: Make a sports card.
Theme: Cultural diversity
Goal: To learn about sports in different countries

At Home

Read about ice hockey in Canada.

> Ice hockey is very popular in Canada. Canadians like it a lot. Ice hockey is exciting. Teams play on a skating rink. Players wear helmets and kneepads. They use hockey sticks and a puck.

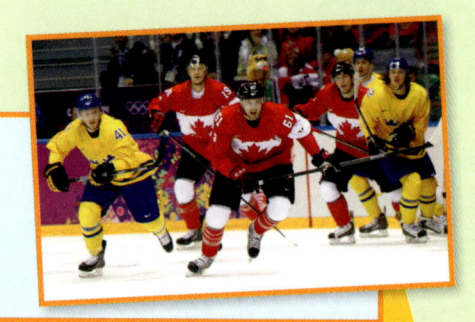

Complete the chart. Use your dictionary and the Internet, if necessary.

Country	Popular sport	Information

Draw pictures or bring photos of the sport to class.

In Class

1. Make a sports card. Use the sample sports card as a model.

2. Tell your group about your sport.

   > Baseball is very popular in Japan. Teams play on a field. They use a . . .

3. Don't show your card to the group. Say the name of your country. The other group members ask questions, and guess the sport.

   > Japan

   > Do they wear uniforms?

   > Yes, they do.

   > Is it baseball?

   > Yes, it is.

4. Display the sports cards in your classroom. Walk around and look at all of them. Vote on the most interesting sport.

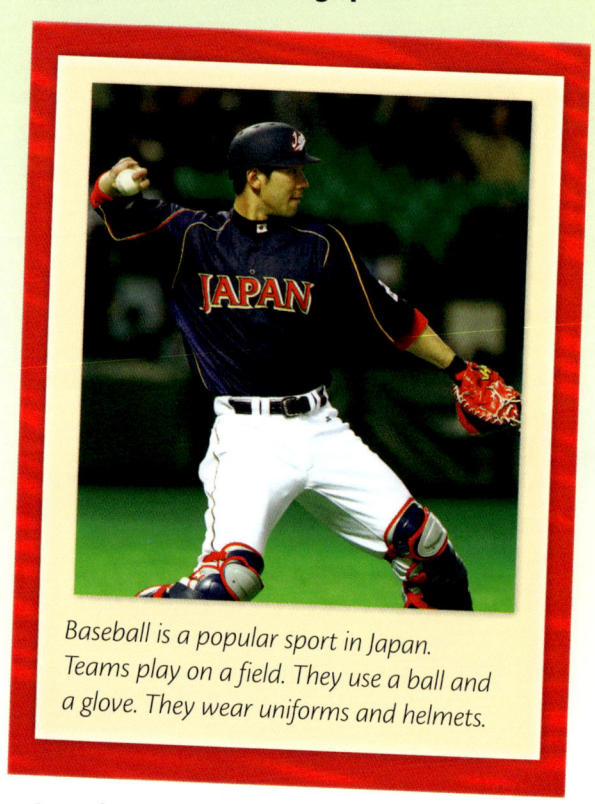

Baseball is a popular sport in Japan. Teams play on a field. They use a ball and a glove. They wear uniforms and helmets.

Sample sports card

UNIT 4

Theme Project: Make a booklet of advertisements.
Theme: Consumer awareness; cultural diversity
Goal: To learn the price of common items in dollars; to share interests

At Home

Read the advertisement.

Hi! I'm Lydia. In my free time, I paint pictures. I need special things for painting. Look at this advertisement from my favorite art store.

Martin's Art Store

Art Supply Sale
Canvas $25.25
Brushes $9.99
Paints $18.70 (each tube)
Easel $129.99

Choose an activity. *My activity is _____.*

What do you need for your activity? Write four items and their prices. Use your dictionary or the Internet, if necessary.

1. _____ 3. _____
2. _____ 4. _____

Draw pictures or bring photos of the items above to class.

In Class

1. Choose a name for your store. Make an advertisement for your store. Use the sample advertisement as a model.

2. Tell your group about the items in your store.

   > I like skiing. Skis are $600.00. Boots are $350.00. A jacket is . . .

3. Give your group's pages to the teacher. The teacher staples together the pages.

4. Pass around the booklet. What equipment and activities are the coolest? Why?

Diego's Ski Store

Skis $600.00
Boots $350.00
Jacket $220.00
Goggles $50.00

Sample advertisement

Unit 4 Theme Project   129

UNIT 5

Theme Project: Make a city guide for tourists.
Theme: Citizenship
Goal: To create awareness of your city or town; to provide information for visitors

At Home

Read about Julie's favorite place in New York.

> Today, I am with my friends at South Street Seaport. There are many things to do here. There are people taking a boat ride. Over there, some people are watching street performers. Right now, we're visiting a museum. It's really interesting.

What are two of your favorite places in your city? Write their names. Then write three things you do in each place. Use your dictionary, if necessary.

Place 1:	Place 2:
1.	1.
2.	2.
3.	3.

Draw pictures or bring photos of the places and the activities to class.

In Class

- Look at all the places. Choose two places.
- Make a page for each place. Use the sample page as a model.
- Choose a group leader. Present your places and activities to another group.

> This is Central Park. These people are walking on a path. These people are . . .

- Give your group's pages to the teacher. The teacher staples together the pages.
- Pass around the guide. What are your favorite activities? Why?

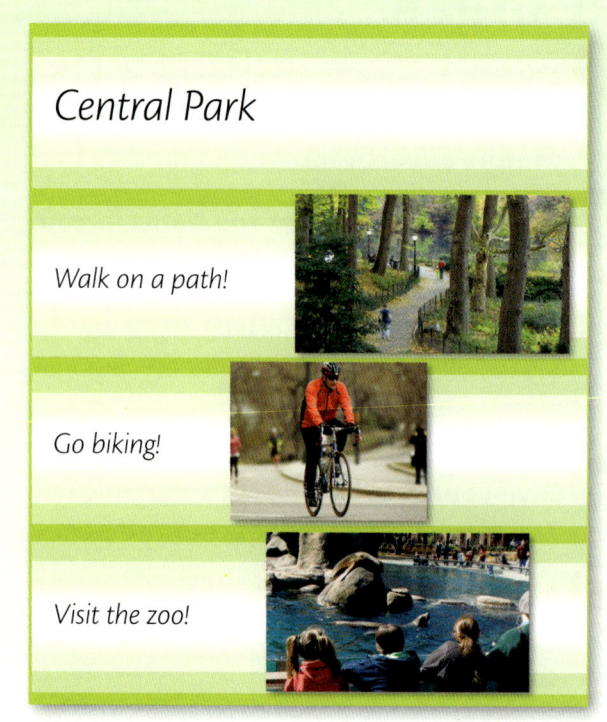

Central Park

Walk on a path!

Go biking!

Visit the zoo!

Sample city guide page

130 Unit 5 Theme Project

UNIT 6

Theme Project: Make a weekend activity poster.
Theme: Relationships; citizenship
Goal: To create stronger relationships in your classroom community

At Home

Read about Hyun's weekend activities.

> I usually relax at home on weekends, but I like to do other things, too. This Saturday, I want to see the new horror movie. I love horror movies. On Sunday, I want to go to a concert with my friends. I want to eat at a restaurant before the concert. Weekends are great!

Write four activities you want to do this weekend. Use your dictionary, if necessary.

1. _____   3. _____
2. _____   4. _____

Draw pictures or bring photos of the activities to class.

In Class

- **Look at all the activities. Choose one activity for each person.**
- **Make a poster. Use the sample poster as a model.**
- **Choose a group leader. Present your poster to another group.**

> Keiko likes to go to concerts. This weekend, she wants to see the Taylor Swift concert. She's awesome!

- **Display the posters in your classroom. Walk around and look at all of them. What do you want to do this weekend?**

Keiko
I want to see the Taylor Swift concert. She's awesome!

Cindy
I want to go to the city nature center. The birds there are beautiful.

Raul
I want to go to a Chicago Bulls basketball game. They're cool!

Sample poster

Unit 6 Theme Project   131

UNIT 7

Theme Project: Make a group menu.
Theme: Healthy food
Goal: To share information about healthy foods

At Home

Read about Home Cooking Restaurant's menu.

Welcome to our restaurant! On today's menu, we have two healthy dishes for lunch. Try our vegetable soup or our chicken sandwich. There are carrots, peas, beans, and onions in the soup. There isn't any mayonnaise on the sandwich – there's only chicken, lettuce, and tomato on it. Both dishes are delicious!

Complete the chart. Use your dictionary, if necessary.

Healthy dish	What's in it?
1.	1.
2.	2.

Draw pictures or bring photos of the foods to class.

In Class

- Look at all the healthy dishes. Choose four dishes. Make a menu. Use the sample menu as a model.
- Choose a group leader. Present your menu to another group.

  > On our menu, we have pasta with sauce. There are tomatoes, onions, and meat in the sauce. We also have a salad. There are carrots, cheese, and lettuce in it. We also have . . .

- Display the menus in your classroom. Walk around and look at all of them. Vote on the healthiest dish.

Menu

Pasta with sauce:
Pasta, tomatoes, onions, and meat

Salad:
Carrots, cheese, and lettuce

Fruit salad:
Bananas, apples, oranges, and grapes

Chicken and vegetable soup:
Chicken, carrots, beans, celery, and onions

Sample menu

UNIT 8

Theme Project: Make an informational poster about a country.
Theme: Cultural diversity
Goal: To learn about different countries around the world

At Home

Read about Peru.

Visit Peru in South America. Go to Lima, an important city in Peru. It's sometimes sunny and cool there. You can go to Machu Picchu from Lima. It's a famous place in the mountains. It's very old and beautiful. You can also see the rain forest in Peru. So, check out Peru. It's a really fun place to visit.

Machu Picchu

Write the information. Use your dictionary, if necessary.

Country: _____
Important city: _____
Famous place: _____
Things you can do: _____
Continent: _____
Weather in that city: _____

Draw three pictures or bring three photos of the things in your chart to class.

In Class

1. **Make a poster. Use the sample poster as a model.**

2. **Read the information on your poster. The other group members guess the country.**

   > This country is in Central America. Cancun is . . .

   > Is it Costa Rica?

3. **Choose a group leader. Present your places to another group. Try to guess the country on each poster. Finally, write the correct countries on the posters.**

4. **Display the posters in your classroom. Walk around and look at all of them. Vote on the most interesting place.**

This country is in Central America. Cancun is an important city there. It's hot and sunny there.

You can visit Chichen-Itza.

You can go to beautiful beaches.

You can listen to mariachi music.

_____
(country)

Sample poster

Word List

Esta lista inclui as palavras e as frases-chave do *Connect Revised Edition* Combo 2. O número que aparece ao lado de cada palavra se refere à página do Student's Book em que elas aparecem pela primeira vez.

Key Vocabulary

Aa
a lot of (54) _____
action movie (78) _____
active (10) _____
activities (37) _____
actually (3) _____
admire (22) _____
adult (72) _____
adventure DVDs (46) _____
afternoon [in the . . .] (39) _____
again (37) _____
age (51) _____
air (110) _____
album (54) _____
all [at all] (11) _____
almost (47) _____
amazing (72) _____
animated movie (78) _____
answer (52) _____
anything (95) _____
apartment building (12) _____
appetizer (94) _____
apple (86) _____
Arabic (106) _____
artistic (8) _____
arts and crafts (38) _____
asleep (70) _____
At least! (109) _____
at night (37) _____
athlete (72) _____
athletic (8) _____
attention (61) _____
average (80) _____
awesome (72) _____

Bb
baby (64) _____
baked potato (94) _____
ball (65) _____
banana (86) _____
barbecue (74) _____
baseball bat (66) _____
baseball player (33) _____
basketball court (5) _____
bass (22) _____
bat [animal] (72) _____
bathing suit (65) _____

beans (94) _____
bear (103) _____
beautifully (76) _____
belt (66) _____
bike path (60) _____
biking (30) _____
bird (102) _____
black bean soup (94) _____
blanket (36) _____
blond (80) _____
boat (60) _____
boat ride (58) _____
body (type) (80) _____
bowling (53) _____
boy band (12) _____
bracelet (66) _____
bread (88) _____
breakfast (16) _____
bring (36) _____
broccoli (86) _____
bug repellent (36) _____
busy (39) _____
butter (86) _____
butter cow (82) _____

Cc
cake (74) _____
camp (36) _____
campers (39) _____
campfire (38) _____
camping (50) _____
canoeing (38) _____
cards (74) _____
carrot cake (94) _____
castle (68) _____
cat (10) _____
catalog (47) _____
cave (102) _____
CD (28) _____
celebrate (74) _____
cents (46) _____
challenges (96) _____
champion (40) _____
checklist (36) _____
check out (26) _____
cheese (86) _____
cheeseburger (94) _____
chicken (92) _____

chicken sandwich (94) _____
chocolate cake (94) _____
circus (72) _____
climb (102) _____
clothes (23) _____
clothing (23) _____
cloudy (100) _____
coat (66) _____
cold (100) _____
collect (18) _____
come (52) _____
comedy (78) _____
comfortable (37) _____
company (26) _____
convenient (54) _____
cook [noun] (75) _____
cook [verb] (38) _____
cookbook (96) _____
cookie (87) _____
cool (100) _____
country (music) (44) _____
creator (26) _____
crossword puzzles (50) _____
cup (88) _____
curly (80) _____
cyclist (33) _____

Dd
dance lessons (18) _____
dancing (50) _____
dangerous (10) _____
delicious (68) _____
dessert (94) _____
die (110) _____
diner (94) _____
dinner (16) _____
dirty (110) _____
discover (46) _____
documentary (78) _____
dog (10) _____
doll (68) _____
dollars (46) _____
download (54) _____
drama (78) _____
dress (37) _____
drinks [noun] (88) _____
DVD (18) _____

Ee
e-books (54) _____
each (46) _____
early (25) _____
easily (8) _____
eat (16) _____
eat out (24) _____
egg (86) _____
egg sandwich (87) _____
electric keyboard (22) _____
else (89) _____
end (81) _____
especially (109) _____
evening [in the . . .] (39) _____
everyone (101) _____
everything (67) _____
exhibit (72) _____
expensive (47) _____
eye (32) _____

Ff
farm (82) _____
fascinating (72) _____
fashion designer (23) _____
feet (32) _____
fence (40) _____
festival (72) _____
few [a few] (89) _____
find (107) _____
fish (94) _____
flashlight (36) _____
float (64) _____
fly (64) _____
follow (61) _____
foot (32) _____
for a change (87) _____
forget (103) _____
fork (88) _____
free time (18) _____
french fries (94) _____
Frisbee (64) _____
fruit (88) _____

Gg
genius (96) _____
German (106) _____
Germany (106) _____
get up (16) _____
glove(s) (32) _____
goggles (32) _____
golf (109) _____
Good! (93) _____
good (at something) (9) _____
go out (24) _____
grade (eighth grade) (21) _____
grades (52) _____
Greece (106) _____
Greek (106) _____
group (44) _____
guess (23) _____
guitar lesson (17) _____
guy (31) _____

Hh
hair (80) _____
hairstyle (80) _____
hand (32) _____
hang out (18) _____
hard [work hard] (23) _____
hardly ever (52) _____
hate (73) _____
head (32) _____
headphones (52) _____
healthy (87) _____
heavy (80) _____
height (80) _____
helmet (32) _____
help [noun] (101) _____
help [verb] (31) _____
high school [adjective] (22) _____
hike (38) _____
hiking boots (36) _____
hip-hop (music) (44) _____
horror movie (78) _____
horseback riding (38) _____
hotel (103) _____
hot spring (102) _____
houseboat (102) _____
how [How old is he?] (3) _____

Ii
ice cream (70) _____
iced tea (94) _____
idea (93) _____
incredible (72) _____
information (101) _____
in-line (skate) (18) _____
instrument (8) _____
interests (50) _____
interviews (26) _____
island (102) _____
Italy (106) _____

Jj
jazz (44) _____
jazz band (22) _____
jazz club (22) _____
jelly (92) _____
jewelry (67) _____
jokes (8) _____
juice (88) _____
just a minute (37) _____

Kk
karate (30) _____
ketchup (92) _____
kind [what kind of] (45) _____
kite (64) _____
knee (32) _____
knee pad(s) (32) _____
knives [*sing.* knife] (88) _____

Ll
language (8) _____
lead singer (12) _____
learn (72) _____
leave (37) _____
lesson (17) _____
lettuce (92) _____
lifeguard chair (65) _____
light (60) _____
line [in line] (60) _____
listen (18) _____
lives (16) _____
long (80) _____
look (like) (81) _____

Mm
main dish (94) _____
make (8) _____
man (64) _____
many [how many] (89) _____
marketing (26) _____
maybe (31) _____
mayonnaise (92) _____
meat (86) _____
medals (40) _____
medium-length (80) _____
melt (110) _____
menu (94) _____
messy (10) _____
midnight (37) _____
milk (88) _____
milk shake (94) _____
million (54) _____
morning [in the . . .] (16) _____
Morocco (106) _____
mountain (102) _____
much [adjective] (45) _____
much [how much] (47) _____
much [very much] (11) _____
music videos (12) _____
musical [adjective] (8) _____
musician (44) _____
mustard (92) _____

Nn
national forest (108) _____
Nature Center (73) _____
nature puzzles (46) _____
near (65) _____
necklace (66) _____
need (33) _____
never (52) _____
No kidding! (33) _____
nothing (87) _____
nutrition (96) _____

Oo
ocean (64) _____
off (to) (36) _____
on time (52) _____
one hundred thousand (108) _____
one thousand (108) _____
only child (40) _____
open (74) _____
or (17) _____

Word List 135

order (95) _____
outdoors (50) _____
over (11) _____
own [his own] (23) _____

Pp
paper airplanes (52) _____
parrot (10) _____
party game (74) _____
pasta (88) _____
pay (attention) (61) _____
pay for (66) _____
peach (68) _____
pepper (92) _____
person (50) _____
pet (10) _____
phone (18) _____
photograph (107) _____
piano (22) _____
piano lesson (19) _____
picnic area (60) _____
picture (8) _____
pie (94) _____
pillow (36) _____
plan [noun] (88) _____
plant [noun] (109) _____
plastic (110) _____
plate (88) _____
play [noun] (68) _____
podcasts (54) _____
poetry (50) _____
police officer (108) _____
pop (music) (44) _____
popcorn (25) _____
Portuguese (106) _____
post (96) _____
potato (86) _____
pounds (82) _____
practice (22) _____
present [noun] (74) _____
presentation (109) _____
pretty (good at) (9) _____

Qq
question (21) _____

Rr
rabbit (10) _____
race car driver (36) _____
radio (36) _____
radio-controlled airplane (46) _____
raft (64) _____
raincoat (36) _____
rain forest (102) _____
rainy (100) _____
read (37) _____
recipe (96) _____
recycle (110) _____
refrigerator (87) _____
reggae (music) (44) _____
relax (74) _____
remember (36) _____

rent (54) _____
review (26) _____
rice (86) _____
ride (58) _____
ring (66) _____
rise (110) _____
river (102) _____
robot (72) _____
role model (40) _____
routine (16) _____
rules (61) _____
run (108) _____
Russia (106) _____
Russian (106) _____

Ss
sail (64) _____
salad (94) _____
salt (92) _____
sand (64) _____
save (110) _____
say (37) _____
scarf (66) _____
science kit (46) _____
scientist (109) _____
score (76) _____
sea (102) _____
seashells (64) _____
sell (54) _____
shop for (66) _____
shopping (50) _____
side order (94) _____
sightseeing (58) _____
skate (18) _____
skateboarder (33) _____
skating [adjective] (23) _____
ski (30) _____
ski boot(s) (32) _____
skier (33) _____
sleep (24) _____
sleeping bag (36) _____
slim (80) _____
slow (75) _____
smart (26) _____
snack (92) _____
snake (10) _____
snowy (100) _____
soap (36) _____
soccer (2) _____
soccer practice (53) _____
soda (94) _____
software (26) _____
something (37) _____
song (49) _____
sound (101) _____
sound (like) (39) _____
souvenir (58) _____
souvenir shop (103) _____
special (12) _____
species (109) _____
spend (time) (50) _____

spider (10) _____
spoon (88) _____
sports equipment (32) _____
stadium (108) _____
stamps (18) _____
stand (60) _____
star map (46) _____
start (77) _____
stay (home) (24) _____
stay on (60) _____
stay up (24) _____
steak sandwich (94) _____
stop (37) _____
stories (38) _____
straight (80) _____
student (22) _____
study (47) _____
sunny (100) _____
sunscreen (36) _____
supplies (88) _____
supposed (to be) (37) _____
sure (79) _____
Sure! (33) _____
surf (30) _____
surfboard (66) _____
surprise (73) _____
survey (19) _____
swim (30) _____
swimmer (33) _____
swimming (51) _____
swimming lessons (38) _____
swim team (33) _____

Tt
take (18) _____
talented (23) _____
talk (18) _____
teach (22) _____
teammates (40) _____
telescope (46) _____
temperature (100) _____
tennis (2) _____
tennis racket (66) _____
ten thousand (108) _____
theater (70) _____
then (16) _____
there [Hello there!] (2) _____
thrilling (72) _____
throw (52) _____
ticket (68) _____
tips (96) _____
today's [adjective] (94) _____
tonight (79) _____
too bad (47) _____
towel (36) _____
traditional (68) _____
trail (103) _____
trash (60) _____
trash can (60) _____
travel vest (46) _____
trip (59) _____

trolley (58) _____
trophy (40) _____
try on (66) _____
twenty-five thousand (108) _____
two thousand (108) _____
typical (12) _____

Uu
underground (102) _____
until (37) _____
us (81) _____
use (18) _____

Vv
vegetable soup (94) _____

video (18) _____
videotape [verb] (59) _____
violin (23) _____

Ww
wait (for) (60) _____
walk (58) _____
wall calendar (46) _____
want (79) _____
warm (100) _____
watch [verb] (16) _____
water (86) _____
water-ski (30) _____
wavy (80) _____

wear (32) _____
weather (100) _____
Web site (12) _____
week (23) _____
weekend (19) _____
weigh (82) _____
win (40) _____
windy (100) _____
wire (82) _____
wolves [sing. wolf] (103) _____
woman (81) _____
work (22) _____
world (40) _____
would (95) _____

Acknowledgments

Connect, Revised Edition has benefited from extensive development research. The authors and publishers would like to extend their particular thanks to all the CUP editorial, production, and marketing staff, as well as the following reviewers and consultants for their valuable insights and suggestions:

Focus Groups

São Paulo **Suzi T. Almeida**, Colégio Rio Branco; **Andreia C. Alves**, Colégio Guilherme de Almeida; **Patricia Del Valle**, Colégio I. L. Peretz; **Elaine Elia**, Centro de Educação Caminho Aberto; **Rosemilda L. Falletti**, Colégio Pio XII; **Amy Foot Gomes**, Instituto D. Placidina; **Lilian I. Leventhal**, Colégio I. L. Peretz; **Adriana Pellegrino**, Colégio Santo Agostinho; **Maria de Fátima Sanchez**, Colégio Salesiano Sta. Teresinha; **Regina C. B. Saponara**, Colégio N. S. do Sion; **Neuza C. Senna**, Colégio Henri Wallon; **Camila Toniolo Silva**, Colégio I. L. Peretz; **Izaura Valverde**, Nova Escola.

Curitiba **Liana Andrade**, Colégio Medianeira; **Bianca S. Borges**, Colégio Bom Jesus; **Rosana Fernandes**, Colégio Bom Jesus; **Cecilia Honorio**, Colégio Medianeira; **Regina Linzmayer**, Colégio Bom Jesus; **Maria Cecília Piccoli**, Colégio N. S. Sion; **Ana L. Z. Pinto**, Colégio Bom Jesus; **Mary C. M. dos Santos**, Colégio Bom Jesus; **Andrea S. M. Souza**, Colégio Bom Jesus; **Juçara M. S. Tadra**, Colégio Bom Jesus.

Rio de Janeiro **Alcyrema R. Castro**, Colégio N. S. da Assunção; **Renata Frazão**, Colégio Verbo Divino; **Claudia G. Goretti**, Colégio dos Jesuítas; **Letícia Leite**, Colégio Verbo Divino; **Livia Mercuri**, WSA Idiomas; **Marta Moraes**, Colégio São Vicente de Paulo; **Claudia C. Rosa**, Colégio Santa Mônica.

Belo Horizonte **Júnia Barcelos**, Colégio Santo Agostinho; **Rachel Farias**, Colégio Edna Roriz; **Renato Galil**, Colégio Santo Agostinho; **Katia R. P. A. Lima**, Colégio Santa Maria; **Gleides A. Nonato**, Colégio Arnaldo; **Luciana Queiros**, Instituto Itapoã; **Flávia Samarane**, Colégio Logosófico González Pecotche; **Adriana Zardini**, UFMG.

Brasília **José Eugenio F. Alvim**, CIL – 01; **Rosemberg Andrade**, Colégio Presbiteriano Mackenzie; **Euzenira Araújo**, CIL – Gama; **Michelle Câmara**, CIL – Gama; **Kátia Falcomer**, Casa Thomas Jefferson; **Almerinda B. Garibaldi**, CIL – Taguatinga; **Michelle Gheller**, CIL – Taguatinga; **Anabel Cervo Lima**, CIL – Brasília; **Ana Lúcia F. de Morais**, CIL – Brazilândia; **Antonio José O. Neto**, CIL – Ceilândia; **Maria da Graça Nóbile**, Colégio Presbiteriano Mackenzie; **Denise A. Nunes**, CIL – Gama; **Suzana Oliveira**, CIL – Taguatinga; **Andréa Pacheco**, Colégio Marista João Paulo II; **Simone Peixoto**, CIL – Brazilândia; **Érica S. Rodrigues**, Colégio Presbiteriano Mackenzie; **Isaura Rodrigues**, CIL – Ceilândia; **Camila Salmazo**, Colégio Marista João Paulo II; **Maria da Guia Santos**, CIL – Gama; **Dóris Scolmeister**, CIL – Gama; **Rejane M. C. de Souza**, Colégio Santa Rosa; **Isabel Teixeira**, CIL – Taguatinga; **Marina Vazquez**, CIL – Gama.

Questionnaires

Brazil **Maria Heloísa Alves Audino**, Colégio São Teodoro de Nossa Senhora de Sion; **Gleides A. Nonato**, Colégio Amaldo; **Gustavo Henrique Pires**, Instituto Presbiteriano de Educação; **Marta Gabriella Brunale dos Reis**, Colégio Integrado Jaó; **Paula Conti dos Reis Santos**, Colégio Anglo-Latino; **Tânia M. Sasaki**, High Five Language Center.

South Korea **Don M. Ahn**, EDLS; **Don Bryant**, OnGok Middle School.

Taiwan **John A. Davey**, Stella Matutina Girls' High School, Taichung City, Taiwan; **Gregory Alan Gwenossis**, Victoria Academy.

Japan **Simon Butler**, Fujimi Junior and Senior High School; **Yuko Hiroyama**, Pioneer Language School; **Mark Itoh**, Honjo East Senior High School Affiliated Junior High School; **Norio Kawakubo**, Yokohama YMCA ACT; **Michael Lambe**, Kyoto Girls Junior and Senior High School; **John George Lowery**, Dokkyo Junior High School/John G. Lowery School of English; **Jacques Stearn**, American Language School; **Simon Wykamp**, Hiroshima Johoku Junior and Senior High School.

Illustration Credits

Ken Batelman 4, 92, 104
Andrea Champlin 95, 119
Laurie Conley 52, 64, 65, 118
Bruce Day 42, 43, 60, 61, 80, 81
James Elston 24, 76, 115
Adam Hurwitz 100, 101

Larry Jones 20, 36, 37, 39, 74, 75, 93
Frank Montagna 16, 21, 47, 70, 77, 84, 98, 99, 105
Rob Schuster 7, 72, 86, 114, 117, 121
Jeff Shelley 10, 11, 15, 49, 56, 73, 90
James Yamasaki 34, 50, 51, 112, 113

Photo Acknowledgements

The authors and publishers acknowledge the following sources of copyright material and are grateful for the permissions granted. While every effort has been made, it has not always been possible to identify the sources of all the material used, or to trace all copyright holders. If any omissions are brought to our notice, we will be happy to include the appropriate acknowledgements on reprinting.

Student's Book

iv (Unit 1): ©Alistair Berg/Digital Vision/Getty Images; iv (Unit 3): ©Score/Aflo/Getty Images; iv (Unit 7): ©RTimages/Shutterstock; iv (Unit 8): ©Danita Delimont/Alamy; p. 5 (TL): ©diego cervo/iStock/Getty Images; p. 5 (TCL): ©David Grossman/Alamy; p. 5 (TCR): ©Mitchell Funk/Photographer›s Choice/Getty Images; p. 5 (TR): ©Purestock/Getty Images; p. 5 (BL): ©Howard Berman/The Image Bank/Getty Images; p. 5 (BCL): ©Jetta Productions/Digital Vision/Getty Images; p. 5 (BCR): ©New York City/Alamy; p. 5 (BR): ©Ira Berger/Alamy; p. 6 (TL): ©Nataliya Hora/Shutterstock; p. 6 (TR): ©Fuse/Getty Images; p. 6 (BR): ©Alistair Berg/Digital Vision/Getty Images; p. 7: ©Josef Hanus/Shutterstock; p. 12: ©Roxana Gonzalez/Shutterstock; p. 13: ©David Livingston/Getty Images; p. 14 (TL): ©Andersen Ross/Blend

Images/Getty Images; p. 14 (BL): ©Jose Luis Pelaez Inc./Blend Images/Getty Images; p. 14 (R): ©Carolin Voelker/Moment Open/Getty Images; p. 17 (L): ©Jose Luis Pelaez Inc./Blend Images/Getty Images; p. 17 (R): ©Kidstock/Blend Images/Getty Images; p. 21 (L): ©sonya_m/iStock/Getty Images Plus/Getty Images; p. 21 (CL): ©Michael CavAn/iStock/Getty Images Plus/Getty Images; p. 21 (CR): ©Judith Collins/Alamy; p. 21 (R): ©Zheltyshev/Shutterstock; p. 22 (TL): ©Santiago Cornejo/Shutterstock; p. 22 (TC): ©Jeff Greenberg 1 of 7/Alamy; p. 22 (TR): ©moodboard/Alamy; p. 22 (BL): ©Radius Images/Getty Images Plus/Getty Images; p. 22 (BC): ©Joey Foley/FilmMagic/Getty Images; p. 22 (BR synthesizer): ©Ingram Publishing/Alamy; p. 22 (BR piano): ©Stockbyte/Getty Images; p. 22 (BR contrabass): ©Horiyan/Shutterstock; p. 23 (T): ©Victor Boyko/Getty Images Wall Street Journal/Getty Images; p. 23 (B): ©eng Li/Getty Images; p. 26: ©Quizlet; p. 27: ©Jetta Productions/Photodisc/Getty Images; p. 28: ©Jon Feingersh/Blend Images/Getty Images; p. 29: ©John Lund/Nevada Wier/Blend Images/Getty Images; p. 30 (baseball): ©Tetra Images/Getty Images; p. 30 (biking): ©Purestock/Getty Images; p. 30 (karate): ©Score/Aflo/Getty Images; p. 30 (skateboard): ©Izf/iStock/Getty Images Plus/Getty Images; p. 30 (ski): ©Mike Chew/CORBIS; p. 30 (surf): ©Holger Thalmann/Stock4B/Corbis; p. 30 (swim): ©stefanschurr/iStock/Getty Images Plus/Getty Images; p. 30 (water-ski): ©Louie Schoeman/Shutterstock; p. 32 (gloves): ©Sandra van der Steen/Shutterstock; p. 32 (goggles): ©Pashin Georgiy/Getty Images; p. 32 (helmet): ©Jiri Hera/Shutterstock; p. 32 (knee pads): ©pryzmat/Shutterstock; p. 32 (ski boots): ©Vadim Ponomarenko/Shutterstock; p. 33 (BL): ©Getty Images; p. 33 (BCL): ©Brett Froomer/The Image Bank/Getty Images; p. 33 (BCR): ©Polka Dot Images/Polka Dot/Getty Images Plus; p. 33 (BR): ©hxdbzxy/Shutterstock; p. 35: ©Fuse/Getty Images; p. 38 (TL): ©Pauline St. Denis/Corbis; p. 38 (TCL): ©Horizons WWP/Alamy; p. 38 (TCR): ©Wilson Goorich/Photolibrary/Getty Images; p. 38 (TR): ©Joos Mind/Taxi/Getty Images; p. 38 (BL): ©Bernd Vogel/Corbis; p. 38 (BCL): ©Don Mason/Blend Images/Corbis; p. 38 (BCR): ©Fotokostic/Shutterstock; p. 38 (BR): ©Johner Images-Bengtsson, Hasse/Brand X Pictures/Getty Images; p. 40 (T): ©Ezra Shaw/Getty Images; p. 40 (B): ©Popperfoto/Getty Images; p. 41 (T): ©Gabriel Rossi/LatinContent/Getty Images; p. 41 (B): ©Monica Schipper/Getty Images; p. 44 (TL): ©Jason LaVeris/FilmMagic; p. 44 (TCL): ©Kevin Winter/Getty Images; p. 44 (TCR): ©Aaron Davidson/Getty Images; p. 44 (TR): ©Roger Kisby/Getty Images; p. 44 (BL): ©Greetsia Tent/WireImage; p. 44 (BC): ©Al Bello/Getty Images; p. 44 (BR): ©Steve Mack/FilmMagic; p. 46 (TL): ©Bayanova Svetlana/Shutterstock; p. 46 (TCL): ©artproem/Shutterstock; p. 46 (TCR): ©Tatiana Popova/Shutterstock; p. 46 (TR): ©Coprid/Shutterstock; p. 46 (BL): ©M.Brodie/Alamy; p. 46 (BCL DVD blank cover): ©olmarmar/Shutterstock; p. 46 (BCL DVD cheetah cover): ©Bildagentur Zoonar GmbH/Shutterstock; p. 46 (BCL DVD space cover): ©ixpert/Shutterstock; p. 46 (BCR): ©Bochkarev Photography/Shutterstock; p. 46 (BR): ©Martins Vanags/Shutterstock; p. 48 (T): ©Photodisc/Getty Images; p. 48 (BL): ©mekCar/Shutterstock; p. 48 (BCL): ©victoriaKh/Shutterstock; p. 48 (BCR): ©Africa Studio/Shutterstock; p. 48 (BR American football): ©kotss/Shutterstock; p. 48 (BR soccer): ©Telnov Oleksii/Shutterstock; p. 50 (L): ©Terry Vine/Blend Images/Getty Images; p. 50 (C): ©Tetra Images/Getty Images; p. 50 (R): ©PNC/Digital Vision/Getty Images; p. 53 (L): ©Wides & Holl/The Image Bank/Getty Images; p. 53 (C): ©Blend Images - Kidstock/Brand X Pictures/Getty Images; p. 53 (R): ©STOCK4B/Getty Images; p. 54 (T): ©Pixland/Getty Images Plus/Getty Images; p. 54 (B): ©Anne Ackermann/Photodisc/Getty Images; p. 55 (T): ©R. Diamond/WireImage/Getty Images; p. 55 (B): ©George Pimentel/WireImage/Getty Images; p. 57 (L): ©photonic 11/Alamy; p. 57 (CL): ©Alexandru Nika/Alamy; p. 57 (CR): ©mekCar/Shutterstock; p. 57 (R): ©DK Limited/Corbis; p. 58 (TL): ©GABRIEL BOUYS/AFP/Getty Images; p. 58 (TCL): ©Richard T. Nowitz/Corbis; p. 58 (TCR): ©Creatas/Getty Images Plus; p. 58 (TR): ©Travelpix Ltd/Photographer's Choice/Getty Images; p. 58 (BL): ©Design Pocs/Ron Nickel/Getty Images; p. 58 (BCL): ©GlebStock/Shutterstock;p. 58 (BCR): ©Andy Sotiriou/Photodisc/Getty Images; p. 58 (BR): ©Steve Vidler/Superstock; p. 59 (L): ©Jack Hollingsworth/Photodisc/Getty Images; p. 59 (CL): ©68/Ocean/Corbis; p. 62: ©Fuse/Getty Images; p. 63 (CL, CR): ©Antagain/iStock/Getty Images Plus/Getty Images; p. 66 (1): ©ZoneFatal/Shutterstock; p. 66 (2): ©Lepas/Shutterstock; p. 66 (3): ©ID1974/Shutterstock; p. 66 (4): ©camilla wisbauer/E+/Getty Images; p. 66 (5): ©vblinov/Shutterstock; p. 66 (6): ©D. Hurst/Alamy; p. 66 (7): ©Antagain/iStock/Getty Images Plus/Getty Images; p. 66 (8): ©-iliadilium-/iStock/Getty Images Plus/Getty Images; p. 66 (9): ©Natthapenpis Jindatham/Shutterstock; p. 68 (T): ©Nic Cleave Photography/Alamy; p. 68 (B): ©MANAN VATSYAYANA/AFP/Getty Images; p. 69 (T): ©Jupiterimages/Photos.com/Getty Images Plus/Getty Images; p. 69 (B): ©bartuchna@yahoo.pl/Shutterstock; p. 78 (TL): ©John Myers/Photolibrary/Getty Images; p. 78 (TC): ©Smokeyjo/Digital Vision Vectors/Getty Images; p. 78 (TR): ©Peter Beavis/Stone/Getty Images; p. 78 (BL): ©Chris Ryan/Caiaimage/Getty Images; p. 78 (BC): ©Joseph Van Os/The Image Bank/Getty Images; p. 78 (BR): ©Warren Goldswain/Shutterstock; p. 82: ©Iowa State Fair; p. 83: ©John Giustina/The Image Bank/Getty Images; p. 88 (1): ©s-ts/Shutterstock; p. 88 (2): ©Tetiana Vitsenko/Alamy; p. 88 (3): ©a-ts/Alamy; p. 88 (4): ©Sinelev/Shutterstock; p. 88 (5): ©objectsforall/Shutterstock; p. 88 (6): ©RTimages/Shutterstock; p. 88 (7): ©Yulia Davidovich/Shutterstock; p. 88 (8, 9): ©Everything/Shutterstock; p. 88 (10): ©Africa Studio/Shutterstock; p. 89 (bread): ©Binh Thanh Bui/Shutterstock; p. 89 (cups): ©Evgeny Karandaev/Shutterstock; p. 89 (fruit): ©Joe Gough/Shutterstock; p. 89 (juice): ©DenisNata/Shutterstock; p. 89 (knives): ©Lai leng Yiap/Collection:Hemera/Getty Images Plus/Getty Images; p. 89 (spoons): ©tratong/Shutterstock; p. 91: ©Comstock/Stockbyte/Getty Images; p. 93 (1): ©Irina Fischer/Shutterstock; p. 93 (2): ©Dusty Cline/Shutterstock; p. 93 (3): ©Stephen Orsillo/Shutterstock; p. 93 (4): © Viktor Fischer/Alamy; p. 93 (5): ©ranplett/E+/Gettty Images; p. 93 (6): ©Feng Yu/Shutterstock; p. 93 (7): ©ajt/Shutterstock; p. 93 (B): ©gcpics/Shutterstock; p. 94 (baked potato): ©Danny E Hooks/Shutterstock; p. 94 (black bean soup): ©adlifemarketing/iStock/Getty Images Plus; p. 94 (carrot cake): ©Brand X/Stockbyte/Getty Images; p. 94 (chocolate cake): ©John Kasawa/Shutterstock; p. 94 (hamburger): ©Gena73/Shutterstock; p. 94 (milkshake): ©Joao Virissimo/Shutterstock; p. 94 (mint tea): ©sirikorn thamniyom/Shutterstock; p. 94 (pie): ©bernashafo/Shutterstock; p. 94 (steak sandwich): ©B & T Media Group Inc./Shutterstock; p. 94 (vegetable soup): ©travelling/iStock/Getty Images Plus; p. 96: ©Jed Share/Kaoru Share/Blend Images/Corbis; p. 97: ©Bob Stevens/UpperCut Images/Getty Images; p. 102 (TL): ©America/Alamy; p. 102 (TC): ©Peter Horree / Alamy; p. 102 (TR): ©Yann Arthus-Bertrand/Corbis; p. 102 (BL): ©Andrew Holt/Alamy; p. 102 (BC): ©Lawrence Sawyer/E+/Getty Images; p. 102 (BR): ©Danita Delimont/Alamy; p. 105: ©Masaaki Tanaka/Sebun Photo/amana images/Getty Images; p. 106 (TL): ©FreeProd33/Shutterstock; p. 106 (TC): ©Radius Images/Alamy; p. 106 (TR): ©Kidstock/Blend Images/Getty Images; p. 106 (BL): ©Photodisc/Getty Images; p. 106 (BC): ©Polka Dot Images/Getty Images Plus; p. 106 (BR): ©Thinkstock Images/Stockbyte/Getty Images; p. 110 (T): ©Denis Burdin/Shutterstock; p. 110 (B): ©Guy Bell/Alamy; p. 111: ©Hero Images/Getty Images; p. 116 (a): ©laura stanley/iStock/Getty Images Plus/Getty Images; p. 116 (b): ©Tetra Images/Getty Images; p. 116 (c): ©Vladislav Gajic/Shutterstock; p. 116 (d): ©Hong Vo/Shutterstock; p. 116 (e): ©EpicStockMedia/Shutterstock; p. 116 (f): ©underworld/Shutterstock; p. 116 (g): ©anopdesignstock/iStock/Getty Images Plus/Getty Images; p. 116 (h): ©emin ozkan/iStock/Getty Images Plus/Gett Images; p. 116 (i): ©titov dmitriy/Shutterstock; p. 116 (j): ©Judith Collins/Alamy; p. 116 (k): ©F1online digitale Bildagentur GmbH/Alamy; p. 116 (l): ©s-cphoto/iStock/Getty Images Plus/Getty Images; p. 116 (B): ©Krivosheev Vitaly/Shutterstock; p. 117: ©nexus 7/Shutterstock; p. 120 (across 2): ©Hurst Photo/Shutterstock; p. 120 (across 5): ©Aheiev Viktor/Shutterstock; p. 120 (across 6): ©gosphotodesign/Shutterstock; p. 120 (across 7): ©Dmitrij Skorobogatov/Shutterstock; p. 120 (down 1 L): ©Nemeziya/Shutterstock; p. 120 (down 1 C): ©Dionisvera/Shutterstock; p. 120 (down 1 R): ©Valentyn Volkov/Shutterstock; p. 120 (down 2): ©pick/Shutterstock; p. 120 (down 3): ©chris kolaczan/Shutterstock; p. 120 (down 4): ©focal point/Shutterstock; p. 120 (down 5): ©Everything/Shutterstock; p. 120 (down 8): ©Brent Hofacker/Shutterstock; p. 123: ©freelanceartist/Shutterstock; p. 126 (T): ©Terry Vine/J Patrick Lane/Blend Images/Getty Images; p. 126 (basket ball): ©Tony Garcia/Image

Source; p. 126 (book): ©Cambridge University Press; p. 126 (cat): ©Swell Media/UpperCut Images; p. 126 (maths): ©Steven May/Alamy; p. 126 (piano): ©UpperCut Images/Alamy; p. 126 (violin): ©Ingram Publishing/Getty Images; p. 127 (T): ©LWA/Dann Tardif/Blend Images/Corbis; p. 127 (B): ©Jeff Morgan 08/Alamy; p. 128 (T): ©Bruce Bennett/Getty Images; p. 128 (B): ©Koji Watanabe/Getty Images; p. 129 (brushes): ©Sergey Skleznev/Shutterstock; p. 129 (easel): ©Comstock/Stockbyte/Getty Images; p. 129 (jacket): ©Victor Nikitin/Alamy; p. 129 (paint tube): ©Piyato/Shutterstock; p. 129 (skis): ©Thomas Northcut/Photodisc/Getty Images; p. 129 (ski boots): ©Anthony Hall/iStock/Getty Images Plus/Getty Images; p. 129 (ski glasses): ©R-O-M-A/Shutterstock; p. 130 (T): ©Panoramic Images/Getty Images; p. 130 (cyclist): ©Spencer Platt/Getty Images; p. 130 (park): ©Demetrio Carrasco/AWL Images/Getty Images; p. 130 (zoo): ©Ellen McKnight/Alamy; p. 131 (T): ©TongRo Images/Getty Images; p. 131 (basketball): ©Gary Dineen/NBAE/Getty Images; p. 131 (bird): ©Medioimages/Photodisc/Getty Images; p. 131 (Taylor Swift): ©Kevin Mazur/WireImage/Getty Images; p. 132 (T vegetable soup): ©Ildi.Food/Alamy; p. 132 (T sandwich): ©FogStock/Alamy; p. 132 (B fruit): ©Africa Studio/Shutterstock; p. 132 (B pasta): ©vsl/Shutterstock; p. 132 (B salad): ©Claudio Baldini/Alamy; p. 132 (B soup): ©bitt24/Shutterstock; p. 133 (T): ©DHuss/E+/Getty Images; p. 133 (band): ©Jeremy Woodhouse/Blend Images/Getty Images; p. 133 (beach): ©Alessandra Bolis/Hemera/Getty Images Plus/Getty Images; p. 133 (pyramid): ©holbox/Shutterstock.

Commissioned photography by Lawrence Migdale for pages iv (Unit 5), 2, 3, 6, 8, 9, 18, 19, 24, 25, 31, 32 (girl), 33 (T), 45, 59 (CR, R), 63 (TL, TCL, BL, BCL, TCR, TR, BCR, BR), 66 (CL, TCL, TCR, TR), 67, 73, 75, 79, 87, 89 (TR), 95, 101, 103, 107, 108, 109.

Cover photograph by ©Henrik Sorensen/The Image Bank/Getty Images

Art Direction, book design, and layout services: A+ Comunicação, São Paulo